SPEEDPRO SERIES

HOW TO BLUEPRINT & BUILD A
4-CYLINDER SHORT BLOCK
FOR HIGH-PERFORMANCE

DES HAMMILL

VELOCE PUBLISHING
THE PUBLISHER OF FINE AUTOMOTIVE BOOKS

Also from Veloce Publishing:

First published in 1997. Reprinted 2000, 2003. Veloce Publishing Ltd., 33 Trinity Street, Dorchester DT1 1TT, England.
Fax 01305 268864/e-mail veloce@veloce.co.uk/web www.veloce.co.uk
ISBN 1-903706-92-0/UPC 36847-00292-3

Typesetting (Soutane), design and page make-up all by Veloce Publishing Ltd.on Apple Mac. Printed in the United Kingdom.

Contents

Veloce *SpeedPro* books -

ISBN 1 903706 76 9

ISBN 1 903706 91 2

ISBN 1 903706 77 7

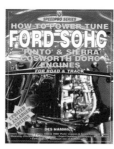
ISBN 1 903706 78 5

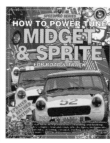
ISBN 1 903706 78 8

ISBN 1 903706 75

ISBN 1 901295 62 1

ISBN 1 874105 70 7

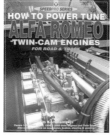
ISBN 1 903706 60 2

ISBN 1 874105 85 5

ISBN 1 874105 88 X

ISBN 1 901295 26 5

ISBN 1 901295 07 9

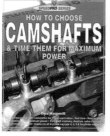
ISBN 1 901295 19 2

ISBN 1 903706 73 4

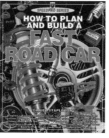
ISBN 1 874105 60 X

ISBN 1 903706 76 1

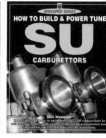
ISBN 1 903706 74 2

ISBN 1 901295 80 X

ISBN 1 901295 63 X

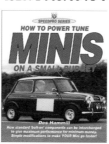
ISBN 1 903706 07 6

ISBN 1 903706 09 2

ISBN 1 903706 17 3

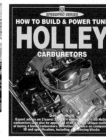
ISBN 1 903706 61 6

ISBN 1 903706 80 7

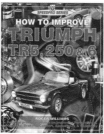
ISBN 1 903706 68 8

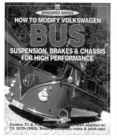
ISBN 1 903706 14 9

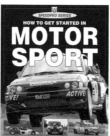
ISBN 1 903706 70 X

ISBN 1 903706 72 6

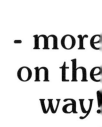

- more
on the
way!

Introduction

This book is designed to give anyone who is rebuilding a mass production four cylinder in-line engine detailed information that will assist them to build the best possible short assembly, within the confines of the parts that are being used. The information provided by this book can also be applied equally well to any standard engine that is being rebuilt and will ensure it gives optimum performance.

The ability of the parts to withstand the rigours of an application is always the main factor in how strong an engine is, but, if the best parts available are not checked for fit and their working clearances are not checked, that engine might last for only a very short time. Most early engine failures are preventable by following the individual part selection and checking procedures and the assembly techniques described in this book.

The majority of engines that are built up for high performance road use can use mainly stock parts and, provided the engine speeds used are not excessive, such an engine will run perfectly well and reliably.

Racing, and other highly stressed competition engines, usually require special components such as forged pistons, heavy duty connecting rods and crankshafts, in order to make them reliable at high rpm.

No matter whether the engine will be for street or track use, or what parts are fitted inside, all parts need to be checked for size, working clearances and accuracy of machining as described in this book.

For high performance use, almost all the clearances used are the maximum within the factory tolerances. For example, if the factory lists a 0.0017-0.0025in/0.046-0.062mm piston to bore clearance tolerance, then standard engines will have clearances at or between these figures. A 'clearanced' or 'blueprinted' engine will use those same factory tolerances but each piston will have 0.0025/0.062mm piston to bore clearance. In some cases, such as crankshaft endfloat, the middle of the tolerance range is used. The 'blueprinted' engine is effectively standard, but selectively so.

With the sizes of the clearances decided on, each clearance must be checked to see if, in fact, the desired clearance is actually present. This process is called 'check fitting'. Each part is checked for fit in a series of dummy partial build-ups long before the engine is finally assembled. After the final assembly, all parts will have been double-checked and the whole engine assembly will be known to have optimal clearances.

With few exceptions, engines are well built originally and give good service, yet after a rebuild often fail for one reason or another. Part failure aside, the most frequent reason for an immediate failure is that somewhere in the engine the working clearances were not correct. The working clearances were no doubt correct with the original parts installed, but when the new parts were installed assumptions were made as to the correctness of the running clearances. The golden rule of engine assembly is to **assume nothing and double-check everything**. If sizes are not checked and clearances not ascertained, a relatively minor clearance discrepancy can lead to the destruction of the entire engine.

All engine parts are built and machined to a particular size but with tolerances on these sizes, so it is quite possible to get a 'stack up' of plus tolerance sizes, which will mean that the particular assembly is tight, or, conversely, a 'stack up' of minus tolerance sizes, which will mean that the clearances will be too loose. It is also quite possible to have a seemingly small single size mismatch which may seem absolutely minor but the ultimate result can still be a major engine failure. Take **no** risks and check **all** sizes and correct any mismatch.

Parts fail for many reasons, but frequently parts that have failed have been used in a high stress situation for far too long where simple replacement would have prevented the failure. A thorough crack test of the offending part and replacement with a new part may have prevented engine failure. Regular maintenance and part replacement is essential in a high performance engine.

Another common problem that leads to failure is using parts that are not strong enough for the rpm that the engine is going to run. Many engine parts will withstand a remarkable amount of stress for a considerable amount of time but will eventually fail, whereas if less rpm had been used, the part would have probably remained in one piece. The solution is to uprate all

A typical mass production cast iron four cylinder block.

of the parts that are known to be not strong enough for the desired engine speed, or reduce the engine rpm.

The majority of conventional mass production four cylinder engines are made of cast iron and are manufactured using 'thinwall' casting techniques, which means that there is sufficient material in all places, but no excess material. This process is designed to give component strength with lightness and reduce costs, but this can only be taken so far, as the last thing a volume producer wants is warranty claims caused by insufficient strength in service. There are now plenty of volume production aluminium blocks which have cast iron cylinder liners. However, the cast iron block is generally regarded as more stable and durable in the final analysis, even if it is slightly heavier. The difference in weight of a cast iron block versus an aluminium block is not as much as might be imagined, as there has to be much more aluminium in the block (cross-sectional thickness) to give comparable strength.

The first consideration about any block is the size of the bores and then the condition of the bores; these factors will ascertain whether the particular block is going to be suitable

for rebuilding. The majority of production blocks will not take overboring beyond the factory recommendation, so the nearer the bore size is to standard, the better.

Rpm limitations

Nearly all mass production four cylinder five main bearing engines are capable of being run up to between 7000 and 8000rpm on a regular basis, up to 8500 with some which have beefy or strutted main bearing caps, **provided the tolerances and running fits are correct**. The main caps and main bearings are not usually the limiting factor unless the caps are very weak. The parts that are not always able to take high rpm are things like pistons, conrods, conrod bolts and some crankshafts.

Pistons

The criteria for piston replacement revolves around the condition of the top ring groove, the size and the condition of the piston skirt and freedom from structural cracks. Any of these problems will mean the piston set (all four) must be changed. Consider the service 'life' of a stock-type cast piston to be approximately 20 to 24 hours of hard use. This means 20 to 24 hours of high rpm operation at elevated temperatures. Note that many factory made performance engines feature uprated pistons and, though these pistons may be of cast type, they look good and go as well as they look.

Factory fitted forged pistons are found in some high-performance mass production engines and can be considered maximum strength items and as good as you can get. Sometimes it's necessary to replace this type of piston with an alternative forging to gain extra piston to valve clearance: the standard piston

A typical set of replacement pistons (cast).

frequently being flat topped with shallow valve reliefs (if any) and not having enough material thickness to deepen the valve reliefs without weakening the piston crown. Note that forged pistons require more piston to bore clearance than cast pistons.

The majority of pistons fitted to mass production engines are of the cast type. The average new cast piston, of any design, is quite satisfactory for use up to 6500rpm in very big four cylinder engines (2500cc), 7000rpm in large engines (1800 or 2000cc), 8000rpm for mid range (1100 to 1300cc) engines, 8000-8500 for small engines (850cc) and pro-rata for other sizes, and will usually give very good long term service under these conditions (20 to 24 hours hard use). The strength of standard pistons is frequently underestimated.

Very modern standard pistons often look like racing engine pistons with narrow section rings and slipper skirts, and are very light and strong. The racing engine of yesterday is now the production engine of today (thank goodness!). Some very modern engines of around 2000cc with these 'racing style' cast pistons, like the Ford Zetec, will stand 8000rpm on an occasional basis (not continuous), while the Vauxhall/Opel 2000 16V with its forged pistons would be good for 9000rpm - if the conrods didn't break at 7500rpm.

Many standard cast pistons do not have an oil slot and the skirt is connected to the piston crown for the full 360 degrees. Such pistons seldom break around the pin boss, but may break in the skirt.

If new cast pistons which have oil slots are used beyond the limit of their strength, the top of the piston simply parts company with the piston pin bosses. This is usually a clean break and will appear as such, with no dark areas which would indicate previous cracks.

Steel strut cast aluminium pistons, while perhaps looking less strong than their straight cast aluminium counterparts (on account of there appearing to be less aluminium connecting the crown to the skirt), are as strong or stronger. The disadvantage with some steel strut pistons is that, after a considerable amount of work, the aluminium around the steel strut or struts cracks. If cracked pistons are used beyond their service life (meaning they have serious cracks) the aluminium skirt of the piston will disintegrate. Some steel strutted pistons are better than others but, overall, the average steel strutted piston will give very good service, although frequent replacement is necessary if reliability is to be assured. The Kolbenschmidt Ford V6 cast aluminium piston (which is steel strutted and can be fitted to the Pinto engine), for example, will withstand 8000 to 8500rpm reliably for a considerable amount of time (say, a season's racing with the engine limited to 8000-8500rpm by mechanical or electronic means). This is not, however, the conventional design of steel strut piston.

Irrespective of the design of the cast piston, the way to ensure piston reliability is to change the set of pistons regularly even if the pistons

measure up and look to be in a serviceable condition. Replace them while they are looking good!

Cast pistons used in a high performance road-going engine which is revved occasionally to high rpm (7000rpm large engines, 7500rpm smaller engines) will normally prove reliable for around 50,000 miles/80,000 kilometres, so long as the engine is well maintained and is fitted with a good air filtration system.

Broadly speaking, consider rpm limits for cast pistons to be -

2500cc - 6000-6500rpm
2000cc - 7000-7500rpm
1500cc - 7500-8000rpm
1000cc - 8000-8500rpm

In many racing applications the range of engine speeds used is quite broad, for instance, 3000-7000rpm (2000cc engine), with between 3000 and 6000rpm being used most of the time. In such circumstances, expect the pistons to last around 24 racing hours. If this same engine was used for continuous 6500-7500rpm operation, forged pistons would be a necessity.

Forged pistons are almost always stronger than any cast piston by way of their design and the fact that the material used in them maintains its strength at the piston's working temperature much better than a standard type cast piston. Forged pistons are more expensive than cast pistons and are essential for pure racing engines constantly turning high rpm. The application determines the type of piston to be used in most instances.

The ability of the piston to maintain optimum performance revolves around skirt wear which controls the piston to bore clearance, which, in turn, controls the attitude of the piston in the bore and affects ring seating. Too much clearance and the piston is able to rock from side to side

Typical cast nodular iron crankshaft.

Typical fully-counterweighted crankshaft.

and the rings will not maintain correct contact with the bore surface so sealing efficiency is lost. The top ring groove in the piston wears out much sooner than the others and, when this groove is no longer on size, or within the tolerance, the piston set must be replaced. There are methods of reclaiming the groove but these are not acceptable for a high-performance engine.

Crankshaft
The crankshafts of most production engines are cast nodular iron and nearly all of these crankshafts are capable of withstanding 7500 to 8500rpm (large engines or small). Many modern engines feature fully counterweighted crankshafts. The advantage of this is reduced vibration and an improvement in engine smoothness, especially at low rpm under load.

Connecting rods
Most standard production connecting

rods are suitable for 6700 to 7500rpm operation, while some standard connecting rods are so good they virtually never break.

Improving a connecting rod's durability can be as simple as fitting uprated bolts, irrespective of the diameter of the bolt concerned, which will improve overall strength of the connecting rod. Fit the best quality aftermarket bolts available.

On many very modern engines the connecting rod I-beam, cap and bolt are too weak for high performance work.

Once the bolts have been uprated, the cap and the I-beam of the connecting rod are the next points of failure, and here the only solution to weakness is to replace the connecting rod with a stronger aftermarket unit.

The connecting rods of most production in-line four cylinder engines will actually stand 7500rpm reliably provided the bolts are replaced with uprated ones. Standard

A range of connecting rod bolts typical of those found in mass production four cylinder engines.

A range of typical original equipment type connecting rods.

production connecting rods are seldom capable of withstanding more than 7500rpm reliably, especially if the I-beam of the connecting rod is of insufficient strength. If the standard type of connecting rod has to be used (competition class rules, for instance), the solution is to use standard connecting rods but to replace them frequently.

Camshaft drives
The majority of modern engines have belt driven camshafts and these drives are very reliable provided the belt is changed frequently. The only uprating that is done to this type of drive is to fit a vernier timing wheel to the camshaft (or camshafts) to achieve precise camshaft timing. Timing belts give consistent camshaft and ignition timing at all revs.

Note that on modified four valve per cylinder twin camshaft engines which have long duration camshafts the piston to valve clearances can become 'tight' (meaning close). The camshaft timing and belt tension must be checked frequently when a new belt is fitted. The reason for this is that the belt, while not actually stretching, does compress slightly (lengthen) and this, effectively, retards camshaft timing. It is not enough to just adjust the tensioner and not check the actual camshaft timing (opening and closing points or full lift positions) because, when the camshafts retard, the exhaust valve heads get closer to the pistons at TDC when the valves are closing. The belt may well have the correct tension after being adjusted but the timing will have retarded. It is possible for the left-hand side exhaust camshaft to have a considerable amount of retardation. To avoid possible piston to valve contact problems on belt drive engines, keep checking and adjusting the belt tension and camshaft timing until you are satisfied that the belt has 'settled.' Always have as much piston to valve clearance as possible on this type of engine, especially for the exhaust valves.

Nearly all camshaft-in-block engines have single row (simplex) chain drives and, usually, a chain tensioner but, unfortunately, standard single row timing chains are not suitable for high-performance use because they wear and/or stretch quite quickly, making replacement a common occurrence if the performance of the engine is to be maintained.

Duplex chain drives are much more effective, provided the chain is replaced when it is showing signs of wear. The range of replacement duplex timing drives is quite large. The principle aim of any camshaft drive is to maintain camshaft and ignition timing accuracy, in relation to the crankshaft, at all rpm. Worn chains, for instance, cause retarded camshaft timing and fluctuating ignition timing.

Chain drive overhead camshaft engines will have either a simplex or duplex chain. Some models of the same engine (performance variants) will be factory fitted with a duplex chain and sprocket set rather than a simplex chain and sprocket set. Always change to the duplex chain and sprocket set if you can. Always fit a top quality new chain, new rubbing blocks and a new tensioner. Some

Typical duplex chain and sprocket set.

overhead camshaft engines were only ever fitted with simplex chains (usually small engines) and this is all that can be used. Expect to have to adjust the timing and to replace the chain regularly in the interests of reliability.

Note that not all duplex chains use a tensioner, even if the original simplex chain did.

Balancing

All engines are balanced by their manufacturers and, although it has to be possible for the odd engine to be slightly out of balance, they are in the minority. The amount of material that is removed when an engine is rebalanced is usually very small. 99.9% of the time, engines are well within the factory tolerance, but there is frequently room for improvement.

All competition engines should be rebalanced. It is usual for some material to be removed from engine components when they are rebalanced, however small. This could be from the connecting rods, pistons, flywheel and the crankshaft, or all of these components. Most connecting rods are within 3 grams weight for weight within a set and within 2 grams end for end. Most pistons are within 2 grams over the set but lightweight replacement pistons could be as much as 100 grams or more lighter than the standard piston.

Oil pump

Stock oil pumps are more than adequate for normal use, and nearly all oil pumps can be uprated to a degree by increasing the relief valve pressure (by packing up the relief valve spring with a spacer or replacing the original spring with a stronger one). There is a limit to the amount of spring tension that can be incorporated into the relief valve spring because, over a certain tension,

the relief valve simply will not release. At this point the oil pressure could exceed 300 pounds per square inch or more. For all four cylinder in-line engines running up to 7500rpm, consider 60-65psi/414-448kpa to be adequate. Avoid oil pressures over 85psi/586kpa.

There is also a limit to what an oil pump can displace and this is ultimately controlled by its capacity. The solution to maintaining more oil pressure is to increase the capacity of the oil pump and, to this end, high volume pumps are readily available. Note that the bearing clearances have an affect on oil pressure; very large bearing clearances can cause low pressure no matter what pump is installed.

Oil pumps wear out and the fitting of a new oil pump (and drive, if applicable) is essential for any high performance engine. Oil pumps have unfiltered oil going through them and particles in the oil cause pump wear. When clearances are increased in the oil pump through wear and tear, the pump's efficiency is reduced.

Sump (oil pan)

The sump will frequently need to be modified by way of increased capacity for high-performance applications. Sumps are improved by increasing their capacity by widening and lengthening the oil reservoir and incorporating a windage tray and a baffle to stop excessive movement of the oil around the oil pick-up.

The depth of the sump is sometimes reduced to improve ground clearance, but there is little point in making the base sump higher than the clutch bellhousing (the lowest point). Reinforce the base of the sump (double skin) to avoid damage to the oil reservoir section of the oil pan (sudden oil loss means a seized

Aftermarket cast aluminium sump (oil pan) which makes a particular front wheel drive engine suitable for rear wheel drive applications.

engine).

Custom made sumps (often cast in aluminium) are readily available from many sources (often including the original equipment manufacturer) to fit virtually any application. There are plenty of specialist companies who deal with one engine and make a range of specialist items, including sumps to fit all sorts of applications. Frequently, the high cost of such items is based on the size of the production run, so it is not surprising the price will be high.

A steel sump can be modified by cutting and welding (mig welding, preferably) a custom fabricated section on to what remains of the original oil pan. Sumps altered like this can be excellent, as steel can be bent and shaped to suit the installation to maximize oil capacity and yet allow things like the starter motor to be accessible. Always reinforce the base of a custom fabricated steel oil pan. Alloy sumps, too, can be modified in a similar manner but they'll need to be tig welded.

Dry sump lubrication systems are available for many engines as a kit and, while being expensive, almost always offer the best lubrication for an engine. The dry sump system is basically only necessary for competition use, but many are found on road-going vehicles used for weekend competition.

DEDICATION

I dedicate this book to Roger Foster of Papakura, New Zealand and Noel Foster of Ramarama, New Zealand, for sparking off my lifelong interest in racing cars. Many years ago, as a child of ten years old, the thrill of being taken for a ride in a 1936 Brooklands Riley Special and then a 1956 D Type Jaguar has never been forgotten ... I distinctly remember Noel telling me not to tell my mother I had been up to100 miles per hour in the D type!

Des Hammil

Using this book & essential information

USING THIS BOOK

Throughout this book the text assumes that you, or your contractor, will have a workshop manual specific to your engine for complete detail on dismantling, reassembly, adjustment procedure, clearances, torque figures, etc. This book's default is the standard manufacturer's specification for your model so, if a procedure is not described, a measurement not given, a torque figure ignored, you can assume that the standard manufacturer's procedure or specification for your engine should be used.

You'll find it helpful to read the whole book before you start work or give instructions to your contractor. This is because a modification or change in specification in one area will often cause the need for changes in other areas. Get the whole picture so that you can finalize specification and component requirements as far as is possible before any work begins.

For those wishing to have even more information on high-performance engine preparation/building/modification, ignition systems and Weber or Dellorto sidedraught carburettors, the following three Veloce SpeedPro titles are recommended further reading. *How to Build Modify & Power Tune Cylinder Heads, How To Build & Power Tune Distributor-type Ignition Systems, How To Build & Power Tune Weber & Dellorto DCOE & DHLA Carburetors.*

ESSENTIAL INFORMATION

This book contains information on practical procedures; however, this information is intended only for those with the qualifications, experience, tools and facilities to carry out the work in safety and with appropriately high levels of skill. Whenever working on a car or component, remember that your personal safety must ALWAYS be your FIRST consideration. **The publisher, author, editors and retailer of this book cannot accept any responsibility for personal injury or mechanical damage which results from using this book, even if caused by errors or omissions in the information given. If this disclaimer is unacceptable to you, please return the pristine book to your retailer who will refund the purchase price.**

In the text of this book **"Warning!"** means that a procedure could cause personal injury and **"Caution!"** that there is danger of mechanical damage if appropriate care is not taken. However, be aware that we cannot foresee every possibility of danger in every circumstance.

Please note that changing component specification by modification is likely to void warranties and also to absolve manufacturers from any responsibility in the event of component failure and the consequences of such failure.

Increasing the engine's power will place additional stress on engine components and on the car's complete driveline: this may reduce service life and increase the frequency of breakdown. An increase in engine power, and therefore the vehicle's performance, will mean that your vehicle's braking and suspension systems will need to be kept in perfect condition and uprated as appropriate. It is also usually necessary to inform the vehicle's insurers of any changes to the vehicle's specification.

The importance of cleaning a component thoroughly before working on it cannot be overstressed. Always keep your working area and tools as clean as possible. Whatever specialist cleaning fluid or other chemicals you use, be sure to follow - completely - manufacturer's instructions and if you are using petrol (gasoline) or paraffin (kerosene) to clean parts, take every precaution necessary to protect your body and to avoid all risk of fire.

Chapter 1
Buying a standard used engine

Ideal sources for engines are breakers' yards or private sellers who are selling components from unroadworthy vehicles. Engines from stock road cars are normally a good choice as the basis of a high-performance unit as they have not been subjected to really high rpm, so the internal parts have never been overstressed. Used factory-built high-performance engines often come from cars which, in their later years, had owners who flogged the engine continuously but never bothered with maintenance. This does not mean that such an engine will be a bad engine, rather that it will most likely need substantial reconditioning because its components have suffered major wear *and* stress.

A common problem with older used engines is their dirty internal condition - caused by a lack of oil and filter changes. Many such engines are coated inside with thick black congealed oil and will require a considerable amount of cleaning

before they can be measured and checked to confirm that the particular short block is suitable for rebuilding and high-performance use.

For very modern engines (say, up to five years old) lubricated by modern oils it takes a considerable amount of abuse to cause major damage to the internal componentry. The chances are that such an engine will be in reasonable condition and require only straightforward remedial work, although the crankshaft journals may need a regrind and the bores reboring.

Many relatively modern engines will have covered a huge mileage and yet the bores could be worn by only 0.001-0.002in (0.028mm-0.050mm); this low wear rate is attributable to the good quality of the engine block material found in modern blocks. Older blocks (pre-1980) do not, as a rule of thumb, fare so well and, being made from 'soft' iron, will be more worn for any given mileage.

The block components to be

replaced as a matter of course in a high-performance rebuild will comprise pistons and rings, big end bearings, main bearings, oil pump, oil pump drive, connecting rod bolts, all gaskets and freeze (Welch) plugs, and, if applicable, camshaft, camshaft bearings, lifters and timing chain and sprockets.

If an engine is bought from a breaker's yard, the breaker will usually give a limited guarantee that the engine is a runner or, if bought for rebuild, that if the block or crankshaft is found to be cracked, as examples, they will replace the faulty components with serviceable items. Make sure such arrangements are clearly established before paying for an engine. Similar arrangements can also be made with private sellers. Despite their somewhat unknown quality, scrap engines are good sources for parts, and, just because a crankshaft is cracked, it does not mean that the rest of the engine is no good.

Frequently having two engines from which to build up one good one is a very good idea as there are twice the number of parts to choose from.

CHECKING ENGINE CONDITION

After purchase, the engine block must be inspected to see if it is suitable for rebuilding for a high-performance application by carrying out the following checks (which do not involve complete dismantling).

With the cylinder head removed, the bores can be checked for size and whether or not the block has a sleeve or sleeves in it.

Caution! - No thin-walled block should be considered for high-performance use if it has a cylinder sleeve or sleeves in it. There are several associated problems with blocks that have had sleeves fitted to them because overall block structural rigidity is reduced and the block's deck can lift/distort under head bolt tension. If a cylinder sleeve is very thin it can crack lengthwise in one or more places and the end result of this can be pieces of the sleeve in the cylinder and a ruined engine. Thin sleeves can become loose through distortion and give poor heat transfer with the likely end result of engine failure. Of course not all sleeves fail, but far too many do and the risk is not worth taking as unsleeved engine blocks are no more expensive.

Some older blocks have quite thick cylinder walls (around 0.312in/8.0mm) and such blocks can have sleeves fitted with few problems because the block's structural rigidity is not significantly affected by the amount machined out of the block when it is bored to take the sleeve. A good sleeve thickness is 0.080in/2.00mm and, when such a sleeve is

pressed into a solid structure, it will give reliable service.

Note that engines that have wet liners (eg. Renault/Alf Romeo) are fine for high performance use, so long as the liners have not been overbored too much in the quest for more capacity.

Blocks which have wet liners fitted to them may be made of cast iron or aluminium. Cast iron blocks are usually found in the less expensive production cars while the aluminium blocks are usually found in the higher priced cars. Cast iron is a much more stable material than aluminium and is, of course, cheaper, which is why it is used more.

When engines with wet liner blocks are cleaned the liners are removed, cleaned and measured. The blocks are then thoroughly cleaned and checked for cracks in the same way as any other block. Check, very carefully, the crankcase area of the block in, and around, where the liners fit. The liners are not structural in these blocks. Any crack found here, however small, means that the block is a write-off because even a small crack is going to get longer. Wet liner alloy blocks are often repaired by welding and then remachining; this might be okay for normal use but **not** for high performance. Unless the block is very rare, look for an alternative sound block and scrap the damaged one.

Wet liner engines have centrifugally cast iron liners which are of excellent quality and the wear resistance of these liners (via the quality of the material) is excellent: many such engines covering 100,000 miles/160,000 kilometers with less than 0.002in/0.050mm of wear in the liners. The liners are always reasonably thick walled with the minimum wall thickness being approximately 0.200in/5.0mm and the

maximum likely to be 0.275in/7.0mm.

If liners are bored out to increase the engine's capacity, the wall thickness will be reduced. Consider the minimum wall thickness allowable to be 0.150in/3.8mm. Do not expect thin walled liners to last forever (they will crack). In the case of racing engines fitted with thin walled liners, cracking of a liner is accepted as a possibility and, as a consequence, liners are regularly checked for cracks.

Not all liners are a uniform thickness all around their circumference. Frequently, when an engine has been enlarged in capacity during its production life by its manufacturer the liners have machined flats adjacent to the next liner for water clearance (0.040in/1.0mm). In such a circumstance a liner may well have as little as 0.135in/3.5mm wall thickness in this area, while the rest of the liner has a wall thickness of, perhaps, 0.160in/4.0mm. If such liners are bored out to take larger diameter pistons, the wall thickness in the areas with machined flats could be reduced to as little as 0.080in/2.0mm. Liners like this do not last long, especially in high compression racing engines pulling big revs. These liners may crack after 250 miles or 400 kilometers of racing. Excessively bored liners almost always crack lengthwise from the top of the liner downward and nearly always in the thin section.

A used engine will nearly always have a bore ridge. This gives an indication of the amount of bore wear but can be misleading because if the engine has been apart previously and had the ridge removed, the bores will appear less worn than they actually are. There is only one way to check the size of the bores and that is to measure them with an inside micrometer. Accurate measurement

Inside micrometer positioned in a bore. Note that the micrometer is being used 90 degrees from the crankshaft axis. The bores wear more in this plane compared to the plane in line with the crankshaft.

emoves any doubt.

Generally, bores that are 0.060in/ 1.50mm oversized from standard and worn are not usually able to be rebored and be reliable in a high-performance application. However, some blocks may still be suitable for reboring with reliability. As an example of an exception to the rule, the Ford 'Pinto' block (Sierra, etc) can be bored out to give a capacity of 2094cc with a 0.088in/2.25mm overbore. Note that many very modern engines will not go more than 0.040in/1.00mm oversize.

Visually inspect each bore for cracks and heavy score marks. Inspect each cylinder in turn while each piston is positioned at bottom dead centre. Use a magnifying glass to check every square inch of each bore for cracks which, if present, will usually be quite visible.

Check the block's deck surface for cracks, especially around the head bolt/stud holes and the areas between the bores, also check that the threads for the head bolts/studs are not stripped. **Caution!** - Do not have a cracked block repaired if the engine is going to be used for a high-performance application, find an alternative crack-free block.

Check the distance from the block

Deck of a block with arrows showing where to check between the bores (all of them) and around bolt holes.

deck to the piston crown with each piston at to dead centre (TDC) - the figure will vary from engine to engine. Scrape the top of the pistons clean near the bore edge so that each measurement will be reasonably accurate. A vernier caliper is accurate enough for this, though a depth micrometer will give a more accurate result. The depth recorded could be anything from 0.004in-0.045in/ 0.1mm-1.1mm. This is a useful figure to know because, if compression is to be increased, planing the block's deck can be one of the easiest methods. Record the figures for future reference.

The replacement pistons may have a higher wrist pin to crown height than those they replace, which will automatically increase the engine's compression. Conversely, the wrist pin to crown height may be less than the original pistons which will reduce the engine's compression. Piston crown to wrist pin heights vary by as much as 0.015in/0.40mm from set to set. Within an individual set variation is usually within 0.002in-0.004in/ 0.05mm-0.10mm.

It's acceptable to remove sufficient material from the block's deck to effectively bring the piston crowns up flush with the deck and, in some cases, above the deck. This can make a considerable difference to CR (compression ratio), especially if 0.040in/1.0mm, or more, can be

removed from the block's deck.

If the bores have large wear ridges they will have to be removed before the pistons can be withdrawn: a ridge removing tool can usually be hired. **Caution!** - Ridge removing tools can actually take out quite a lot of material and, if the bore is excessively worn, by the time the ridge has been removed the bore may well require a second oversize rebore instead of the first oversize rebore. Keep this fact in mind when using a ridge removing tool.

Check each main bearing cap for markings so that there is no doubt as to which way around the cap went or what number it is. Mark each main cap if necessary.

Check the numbering of each connecting rod. Some manufacturers do not number the connecting rods at

A typical set of main caps. Each has its correct number cast into it and the arrow on the top shows which way around the cap goes. Numbering is 1 to 5 from the front of the block backwards.

all (most do). The factory marking is not always that clear and often the numbers are incomplete. Mark or remark the connecting rods if necessary. As an additional aid to reassembly, stamp the connecting rod's numbers into the block rail. This means that as each connecting rod's numbers face the block rail that same number is stamped there, making it virtually impossible to put a connecting rod and piston in the wrong way around. It also makes it easy to see

Connecting rod numbers stamped on the connecting rod and the same number stamped into the block rail.

rod bolts. The tubing will protect the crankshaft journal surfaces from the connecting rod bolt threads as the pistons and connecting rods are withdrawn from the block.

The flywheel bolts can be undone at this point. Mark the position of the flywheel in relation to the crankshaft. Two adjacent dots (one on the crankshaft and one on the flywheel)

Here both main cap and block surface are numbered. While not absolutely necessary for identification, it's good practice and removes all doubt as to which way around and where the parts fit.

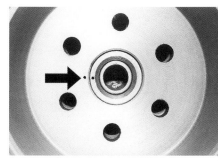

Two dots mark the relative positions of crankshaft and flywheel.

A piece of wood jammed between the crankshaft and the side of the block will allow the flywheel bolts to be tightened without risk of damage to the crankshaft.

that the pistons are in correct order.

There is some variation in how connecting rod caps are secured. It may be that the connecting rod has bolts firmly fitted into it and the cap is located by these bolts and nuts are used to secure the cap. Alternatively, caps can be located and secured by two small dowels and bolts screwed into the connecting rod. Some engine designs use serrated partline faces and two bolts to locate and secure the connecting rod cap.

Undo, and then remove, the connecting rod nuts/bolts and lift the cap away from each connecting rod. Use a small copper hammer to release the cap by alternately tapping each side. With the cap off, place a 2-3in/ 50-75mm length of clear plastic fuel hose on the protruding threads (if applicable). The tubing should be a reasonably tight fit, so expect to have to screw the tube onto the connecting

for the purposes of alignment are sufficient. Even if the flywheel can only go on in one position two extra dots can still offer quick visual verification.

The use of a 2 x 1in or 50 x 25mm piece of wood is ideal to lock the crankshaft in position so that tension can be applied to the flywheel bolts to undo them. Place the piece of wood between the rear cylinder's connecting rod journal and the crankcase.

If not already clearly numbered, number each of the main bearing caps.

Undo the main cap bolts and remove the main caps one by one. When the bolts have been removed,

use a copper hammer to lightly tap each side of the main cap until it lifts out of the block register. With all main caps removed, lift the crankshaft out of the block keeping it parallel to the block.

There is some variation in the method of cylinder block main cap bearing location. The majority of modern engines have the main cap fitted into a register. This means that the cap is a tight fit into the block, ensuring no sideways movement of the cap is possible during service. **Caution!** - If the fit is not tight, the cap

Modern engine designs use register location for main caps.

An older design of main cap (though still in production) which uses hollow dowel location.

Main cap sitting on the edge of the block register. The cap should not go in unless it is 'snapped' in.

Main cap being lightly tapped into the register. As illustrated, a copper hammer is ideal for this.

usually a mismatch of approximately 0.030in/0.75mm. An example of this sort of location method, combined with a complete lack of numbering, is the previously mentioned "A-series" engine which is of three bearing main cap design: each cap is a different shape and the dowels are offset.

It is not possible to assemble an engine with a main cap around the wrong way or have a cap fitted to the wrong set of dowels and still end up with a crankshaft that will rotate freely.

The tunnel sizes of the mains can be checked after the caps and registers have been thoroughly cleaned and the caps reinstalled. With the bearing shell inserts removed from the block and caps, start with the rear most main and fit the cap into the register and 'snap' it in using a copper or plastic hammer. Using cleaned bolts, torque the bolts to the prescribed setting and measure the inside diameter of the tunnel with an inside micrometer. Repeat the process for the other caps. Compare the measurements with the factory specified tolerances which are available from engine machine shops.

Caution! - Any block that is being prepared for high-performance use and which has its camshaft in the block, **must** have the camshaft bearings replaced. Camshaft bearings do not last forever, and the clearances between the journal and the bearings can become excessive (a source of oil pressure loss).

Summary of checks

Check the bores for wear.
Check the bore sizes for suitability for reboring (0.060in/1.5mm oversize is the usual maximum).
Check for obvious cracks in all bores and all over the block.

s not located properly and sideways movement is quite possible which may well result in a main bearing failure. If a ap simply drops into position, the block is **not** serviceable.

Older engine designs often eature hollow dowel main cap ocation (the Austin/Morris/MG/Rover "A-series" engine for example) or plain dowel location. The cap is positively located, but this is not as good a system as the register type. Caution! - The caps must be a tight fit onto the dowels which means that hey must not fit by hand pressure alone. If a cap simply drops onto the dowels, the block is **not** serviceable.

Dowel located main caps will be numbered or the dowels will be offset, which means that if a cap is put on the wrong way around the tunnel bore will most certainly not be round - there is

Check for damaged head bolt/stud threads and the main cap bolt threads in the block.
Check the main cap registers for 'snap in' fit or tightness of fit on the dowels.
Check the tunnel bore diameter of each main bearing against known factory tolerances.
Check that all main caps are clearly numbered.
Check that all connecting rods are clearly numbered at the part line.
Stamp the connecting rod numbers on the block rails for ease of assembly.
Have the crankshaft 100% crack tested.
Have the conrods 100% crack tested.
Have the block crack tested. In this instance, 100% of all bores, main bearing webs and caps.

Chapter 2
Buying a used high-performance engine

Potentially, one of the worst engines to buy is an already rebuilt and modified one that has been used in a high-performance environment, like racing or rallying, but has an unknown history. Such an engine may have been stripped and rebuilt with new bearings, rings and gaskets, but it may not have received a thorough inspection and crack testing of all of the essential components and, often, bores will be worn - the engine will never make top power in such condition.

Far too often, high-performance engines are sold when they are worn out and in dire need of a rebuild and major part replacement. These engines seldom pass even the most rudimentary inspection. It's often amazing to see what has been done to resurrect a part of an engine in an effort to make it serviceable enough to get rid of ...

Of course not all secondhand high-performance engines are bad

engines, but they can be a risk. What starts out as a very reasonably priced unit can end up needing a considerable amount of money spent on it to put it right or, worse, may be a complete write off in the final analysis.

There is always the honest sale, when an engine has been rebuilt correctly and when sold on gives good reliable service to the new owner. Make the seller prove to you that the engine being sold is a good one. This can be done to a certain degree via a partial strip down and does mean removing the cylinder head and sump (oil pan) and checking the condition of the bores and the bottom end of the engine generally. With the complication of twin camshaft engines, and the cost of some head gaskets, this procedure may not be a viable option but, nevertheless, it's the only way to be sure that the engine is really okay.

Many people will not touch a used high-performance engine and

instead build a 'new' engine in spite of the high initial cost - experience has shown them that it is less expensive in the long run, and at least you know what you've got!

You can ask to see receipts for boring, grinding, surface grinding, crack testing and parts that went into the engine. If the work has actually been done the seller will usually offer all receipts as proof. Check with the engine machine shop which did the work to verify that what is claimed to have been done was, in fact, done on the engine in question.

Engine machine shops perform the tasks requested by the customer on the parts supplied and frequently have no idea of the service history of those parts. The engine machine shop can only verify that the parts were remachined by them for a particular customer. For example the connecting rods in an engine could have been refurbished totally with resized big ends, new bolts, straightness tested and crack tested and be regarded as rebuilt. If stock connecting rods have been in a performance engine previously and subjected to severe stress there is no telling how long they will last. The connecting rods may well give further good service but there is a high risk factor attached to their re-use. So there is more to this than just remachining parts. **Caution!** - Beware of standard production connecting rods that have been used in an engine subjected to sustained high rpm, or be prepared to change them if their history cannot be verified.

Take nothing for granted and check to find out as far as possible exactly what was done to the engine, and then check with a partial strip down that the parts claimed to be in the engine are, in fact, fitted to the engine you are wanting to buy. The time to find out all about the engine in question is before the money is handed over, not after.

WHAT TO CHECK IN UNUSED/ REBUILT ENGINES

With the cylinder head removed, each bore can be checked for size at top dead centre, mid stroke and bottom dead centre. This entails using inside micrometers. The condition of the bore walls can be inspected with checks made for score marks, cracks, porosity and possible bore damage from previous engine problems. It is reasonably easy to check whether the bores have been freshly remachined or simply rehoned. Freshly bored bores are 100% shiny from top to bottom and on size, while rehoned bores never have quite as good a finish as it is very difficult to remove all marks that indicate prior use without losing the parallelism of the bore or ending up with too much piston to

bore clearance.

The oil pump can be looked at to see if it is new, and also whether it is standard or high volume. The oil pump drive, or gear, can be checked to see if it is new. Oil drives vary, but all have contact areas where the rotary motion is transmitted and it is these surfaces that will show signs of wear. Any rebuilt engine should have a new oil pump drive (if it is a separate item). The drive fitting on the distributor spindle and into the oil pump must also be in serviceable condition.

The camshaft (if block located) can be looked at with an inspection light to see whether it is new or used and whether it has any worn lobes. The lobe flanks can be looked at for surface marks and possible disintegration of the surface. Check visually the nose of each lobe for surface scuffing and consider using a dial indicator and stand to check the amount of lifter (tappet) rise (lifter in situ) and check this against the camshaft card (specification supplied by the cam manufacturer). At the very

A lobe of a used camshaft that is still in serviceable condition. Note that the wear pattern (shiny surface) on the toe of this lobe is more pronounced on one side than the other.

least all of the inlet lobes should give the same reading and all of the exhaust lobes should give the same reading. New camshafts are "Parkurised" (blackened appearance) while used camshafts will be partially polished via the lifter contact.

Note that a camshaft lobe is not parallel ground across the lobe, but is slightly tapered to match the base of the lifter. The lifter is positioned in the block so that approximately half of the lifter is in contact with the lobe. This offset placing of the lifter promotes lifter rotation.

The connecting rod side play can be measured with a feeler gauge. This is achieved by moving the connecting rod sideways and inserting a feeler gauge between the big end and the crankshaft face. Beware of excessive side clearances (0.009in/0.225mm plus) as this will allow too much sideways movement.

Each connecting rod bearing cap can be removed and the journal size and surface condition checked, as can what type of shell is fitted and whether it is new or not. A feeler gauge (approximately 0.006in/0.15mm) should be inserted in between the connecting rod side and the crankshaft when a connecting rod's nut/bolts are undone to prevent any movement of the connecting rod when the turning torque is applied. This is to prevent

Feeler gauge positioned between the connecting rod and the crankshaft's big end journal side face.

Checking crankshaft endfloat. The crankshaft is moved forward with a large screwdriver so that the thrust face of the crankshaft is hard up against the main bearing thrust surface. Whatever size feeler gauge can fit in the gap is equivalent to the endfloat present.

any damage to the bearing shell insert.

The crankshaft's endfloat can be checked with a feeler gauge This is achieved by pushing the crankshaft backwards or forwards and inserting the right sized feeler gauge into the available gap. Further to this, the rear facing thrust surface or surfaces of the thrust bearings wear (clutch pressure) so the clearance may well be at or near the top limit of the factory tolerance. If the gap is excessive (over the maximum size) further investigation will be required to check that the actual crankshaft thrust surface is not worn out. If the crankshaft thrust surface is worn more than 0.002-0.003in/0.05-0.07mm and

oversized thrust washers are not available for the engine, the crankshaft is a write off. Oversize thrust washers are usually available.

Note that any crankshaft thrust surfaces that are reground must be smooth (same as a journal surface). The side of the grinding wheel is not continually redressed like the front of the wheel is and it will seldom give a perfect finish. This means that the crankshaft's thrust surfaces may not be smooth enough and the thrust surfaces of the bearings will wear very quickly. If the reground surfaces are not perfect, do not use the crankshaft; get a replacement.

The main bearing caps can be removed in turn and the journal surfaces checked for condition and what type of bearing shells are fitted and whether they are new or not. Check the shells for score marks and dirt particles.

The main caps should have remained firm in the block registers after the bolts were removed. The main caps have to be tapped alternately on each side to release them from the register. If the cap can be simply lifted off the block, that main bearing cap is loose in its register and will have to be repaired. The amount of looseness may not be much but any

looseness is not acceptable. Frequently a 'sprung' bearing cap is only loose by 0.001in/0.028mm but this is too much. All main bearing caps must have a positive 'snap in' fit into the block register.

Older engine designs with dowel located main caps must be a tight fit onto the dowels. Main caps of any sort must be positively located and to rely on the bolts or studs and nuts to accurately locate the cap is not acceptable.

Although checking an engine in the manner described cannot remove all possible doubts as to its condition, it will certainly pick up obvious defects and potential problems that would otherwise have remained hidden until after the sale had been made.

Agree with the seller before partially stripping the engine that if the engine is exactly as is claimed you'll buy it in its partially stripped condition or, if it isn't, you'll not be taking the engine and the seller will have to reassemble it. If the engine will stand the inspection the owner will not object to the partial strip down because, after a small amount of work the engine will have been sold and at no additional cost to the seller.

Chapter 3
Choosing replacement parts

PISTONS

There is a huge range of cast aluminium replacement pistons available for all of the common in-line four cylinder engines. Replacement pistons are made in many countries and to similar standards. Some pistons are stronger than others, but virtually all standard cast pistons will withstand sustained revs of 7500rpm (1000cc, or smaller), 7000rpm (1500cc), 6500rpm (2000-2500cc). Brand new cast pistons will last 1000 racing miles/1600 racing kilometers. Using cast pistons longer in a racing engine is accepting risk of breakage. Revolutions higher than those mentioned should not be considered sustainable for cast pistons.

Average standard (stock) pistons are not weak, it's just that they have a design limit beyond which it is unreasonable to expect them to go. The usual result of over revving a stock type cast piston (one with oil slots) is that the piston crown parts company with the rest of the piston or, if the piston has oil drain back holes drilled in the oil groove and the crown is integral with the piston skirt, the skirt will break. Some very modern engines have pistons that look just like racing pistons and have top quality piston rings: they are really very good.

If a cast piston remains in one piece, the top ring groove wears out along with the piston skirt (creates excessive piston to bore clearance). The solution for the prevention of piston failure when stock cast type pistons are being used is to change the pistons frequently (at every rebuild).

Cast pistons

The material from which pistons are constructed does vary, but most manufacturers make their product to meet the original factory specifications and standards. The design of aftermarket replacement piston may vary from the original equipment part in that some original pistons have steel struts, while the replacements do not and vice versa. The steel strut piston may actually look a bit weaker because it has less aluminium joining the skirt to the crown, but this is misleading. Steel strut pistons are very strong and what usually happens after a lot of use is that they develop cracks in the aluminium around the steel strut. Frequently, steel strut cast pistons do not do sufficient work to crack unless the pistons have been

A steel strut piston which has two oil slots milled in through the oil ring groove. Unless unusually strong, such pistons need frequent changing if over 7000rpm is used on a regular basis.

The underside of a cast aluminium piston (not steel strut) which has holes drilled from the oil ring groove to the underside of the piston. Such a piston will withstand use up to 7500rpm, or more, but needs replacing at each rebuild.

subjected to extreme operating conditions.

The 100% aluminium piston will usually have more substantial ribbing connecting the gudgeon (piston pin) pin bosses to the piston crown (as compared to steel strut piston) and may appear to look a lot stronger. If there are several manufacturers making suitable replacement pistons, look at the underside of the piston and check to see how substantial the ribbing is. The thicker the ribbing, the stronger the piston - all other things being equal.

Cast pistons will only stand sustained (being taken to the maximum revs already mentioned at every gearchange) high rpm use for so long and should not be expected to withstand sustained elevated temperatures for long periods. Their strength when hot is significantly less than that of a forged piston. With CR (compression ratio) up to 10.75:1 and rpm not exceeding 7000-7500 or so, cast pistons running with suitable piston to bore clearance can give very reliable service even for motorsport but **frequent** piston replacement **is** necessary. In short, sustained high rpm with full load conditions requires the use of forged pistons but, up to that

point, cast pistons can give very good service. Forged pistons are not normally necessary for road going vehicles.

In motorsport use replace standard-type cast pistons whenever the crankshaft bearings are changed. If the oil pressure reduces because of wear and tear (not damage)

Dimension 'A' is parallel down to the bottom of the oil ring groove and is generally 0.012in/0.30mm less than bore size. Dimension 'B,' taken beneath the bottom of the oil ring groove, is approximately 0.003in/0.076mm less than the bore size and dimension 'C,' taken at the base of the skirt is usually between 0.002-0.025in/0.05-0.06mm less than the bore size. Most stock piston to bore clearances when new are 0.0015-0.002in/0.03-0.05mm. The factories make them reasonably "tight" for average street use.

necessitating new bearings to restore the clearances, the engine has obviously been subjected to some use and it is time to replace the cast pistons, too. This regime may sound excessive but, in actual fact, it's quite reasonable.

Note that the top area of a piston (where the rings are situated) is round, but the skirt is tapered and the piston body is ground oval. Piston diameter is measured at 90 degrees from the wrist pin and at the bottom of the skirt.

The compression seal is dependent on the fit of the compression rings in their piston grooves. The side clearance between

the ring and the piston groove is usually about 0.001in/0.028mm: consider that when this gap becomes 0.002in/0.05mm (measured with a new ring fitted), or more, through wear, that effective compression sealing has been lost and replace the piston set. Grooves can be restored by machining out the groove to a new size (a combination of the ring thickness, a steel spacer thickness and the running clearance); the steel spacer fits at the top of the combination (nearest the piston crown). **Caution!** - This method of repair is reasonably satisfactory for a road car, but **never** for a high-performance engine.

Forged pistons

Forged pistons will always maintain the top ring groove size longer than a cast piston because their construction material is not as 'soft' at the piston crown's operating temperature, and most also have narrow section rings fitted which are lighter. Forged pistons dissipate heat better than most cast pistons. One advantage of the cast piston over the forged piston is that it requires less piston to bore clearance and, in a high-performance street engine, for instance, this will mean quieter operation, better ring seal (less piston rock) and frequently more power. High performance street engines work from idle (1000rpm) through to perhaps 6500rpm much more than they do from 6500rpm to 7500rpm. If an engine is not going to be constantly turning high rpm, cast pistons are the better option.

The construction of a forged piston differs from that of the cast piston. Forged pistons usually have a series of holes drilled through the oil ring slot and into the underside of the piston (but not always). The forged piston is partially stronger because of

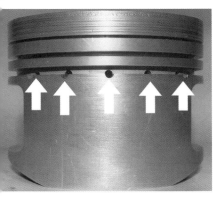

A forged flat-topped piston. Note the holes in the oil ring groove for the draining of oil. On this particular piston, the holes are partially in the skirt.

his design feature when compared to he cast piston which has two milled lots in the oil groove for oil draining. Lightweight forged pistons are the best option for a high revving engine and vill withstand up to, and in excess of,)500rpm.

PISTON RINGS

Top ring

The most common type of eplacement top ring is the high quality cast iron ring (actually a special alloyed material). These rings do not offer the same wear characteristics as moly or

Underside of a forged piston. The top of the piston is fully connected to the skirt unlike cast pistons.

chrome plated rings and are not suited to high-performance engines where maintaining the end gap size is vitally important. Forged pistons almost always feature narrow section compression rings and two or three piece oil control rings. Many modern standard production engines now feature moly top compression rings. The ring sets of some standard production engines are capable of high rpm motorsport use (Ford Zetec rings, for example).

The top ring wears the most because it is subjected to much more heat than the second ring. When engines are assembled new, they are set with a particular ring end gap. As the circumference of the ring wears in use the ring gap naturally gets larger and this contributes to a reduction in

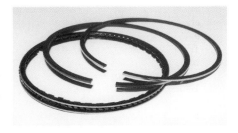

Typical ring set comprising single moly top rings, cast iron second rings and a three-piece oil control ring set with chromium plated rails and a circumferential expander.

compression.

The top ring also wears on its width and, as its width reduces from stock, the ring is no longer a good fit in the groove of the piston and compression sealing is lost. Once there is 0.001in/0.028mm of measurable wear (using a micrometer) from the original size, it's time to replace it. Many modern engines have narrow top rings, just like those found on forged racing pistons.

Chromium plating of the top ring face (the one that contacts the bore) resists dirt becoming embedded in that

A micrometer positioned correctly for the accurate measurement of a used piston ring.

surface of the ring. A chrome ring is still basically a high quality cast iron ring, but it has a very hard wearing face. Chromium plated top compression rings resist circumferential wear which means that the ring's end gap is maintained for the effective life of the ring. Chrome rings can be difficult to seat, in that they can take quite a while to "bed in."

Moly rings are high quality cast iron rings with a molybdenum segment in the edge that is in contact with the bore. Molybdenum is a wear resistant material and these rings certainly wear very well. They seat very quickly (basically instantly), hold the end gap and are very easy on the bore. They are good rings to use and highly recommended. Some stock engines use a top 'Moly' ring.

Note that conventional rings which have been subjected to severe overheating (short of seizure) lose their tension and, when this happens, nothing can be done other than replace them. The ring is no longer exerting sufficient pressure on the bore wall. The engine will run fine, burn no oil, but will not have good power (lacks compression seal). A leak down tester will always find this fault, but a standard compression tester will not.

End gap of a ring being measured at the top of a good (on size) bore which is not worn in any way. Ring wear is radial and it doesn't take much wear of the contact surface to cause the ring end gap to open up considerably.

View of an assembled three-piece oil control ring set up clearly shows the construction of the ring.

Second ring

Second rings are made of good quality cast iron and, as they do not get quite as hot as the top ring, generally retain their tension far longer than a top ring. The second ring groove of the piston also does not wear to anything like the extent of the top ring groove. Second compression rings are generally trouble-free: wear being measurable at the end gap of the ring and the width of the ring.

Note that because not all of the ring is encapsulated in the groove of the piston, a portion of it does not wear. To measure the true thickness of a ring, the micrometer is positioned on the inside of the ring and the anvils of

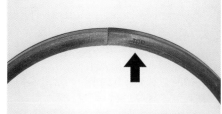

Word 'TOP' marked on this top ring which indicates the right way up for the fitting of the ring.

the micrometer must not go over two thirds of the width of the ring's section.

Three-piece oil control ring

One of the best oil control rings (effectively the only type of oil ring to use these days) and now universally used is the three-piece one which has two chrome plated rails and circumferential expander. The expander holds the two rings in place and also exerts radial pressure on the two rails so that they are held against the bore wall under tension. These oil control rings are very efficient and are generally available for all engines. Both cast and forged pistons use this type of oil control ring and for all applications. One-piece oil rings with an expander are also available and they work very well, but the one-piece oil control ring which has no expander is not suitable (not efficient enough) for use in modern engines.

Always read the instruction sheet from the replacement ring manufacturer because many first and second rings, although looking similar, are, in fact, quite different. It depends on the type of ring, but most top rings have a right way up fitting position which is usually indicated by two indent marks near the gap which must be upward when installed on the piston.

The oil ring is not critical, other than that the expander must butt up correctly before the rails are fitted

because the ring combination cannot be installed correctly otherwise. If the expander is damaged the rails may not have any tension on them. If this happens the oil will go straight up past the rings and into the combustion chamber.

Summary

The fitting of a "single Moly" top ring, a plain second ring and a three-piece oil control ring is the recommendation for any high-performance engine. This combination is now basically the standard in the motor industry.

MAIN & CONNECTING ROD BEARINGS

Available bearings range from plain white metal to heavy duty triple metal bearings. The plain bearings will not last as long as heavy duty bearings, but they are more forgiving. If dirt particles get into the engine's oiling system, those particles will embed themselves into the surface of the plain bearings and, although the situation is far from perfect, the effect of the abrasive action of those particles on the crankshaft journal surfaces is very much reduced. The use of heavy duty bearings is, however, always recommended for high-performance use.

If dirt gets into the oiling system in an engine equipped with heavy duty bearings, the particles will not embed themselves completely in the surface of the bearing shells as the shells are too hard. The result is that the particles spread around the bearing shell and wear the crankshaft journal out rapidly and generally make a real mess of the engine. In this situation with the usual non-hardened crankshaft fitted, the crankshaft will wear out quite quickly.

A hardened crankshaft will resist journal wear to a high degree, but

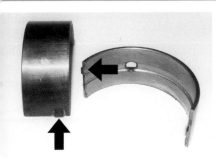

One bearing set of main bearing shells with the location tabs clearly visible.

here is a limit. Under normal circumstances metal particles do not get into the engine's oiling system and heavy duty bearings give better service meaning maintain the working bearing clearance with no reduction in oil pressure) with longer periods between bearing changes.

All bearing manufacturers make bearing shells to exacting standards. The main difference is in the material used in the bearing which affects the load carrying capacity of the bearing, and the time the bearing can take the load before losing required clearance (wears out).

All crankshaft and big end bearing shells have tabs on them for location into the engine block tunnels and the conrod tunnels. These tabs will not stop the bearing shells from rotating in their tunnels; they are purely an assembly aid. If bearings 'spin' in a block it's because the tunnel size is too large and no longer exerts any 'crush' on the bearing halves. Crush is very easy to check during assembly.

CAMSHAFT BEARINGS (IN BLOCK CAMS)

These bearings are an interference fit in the block tunnels and they're fitted into the block using a mandrel. The bearings vary in outside diameter and must be size matched to the correct tunnel to be able to be fitted

successfully.

Camshaft bearings are not subjected to the same wear as main or connecting rod bearings, but the bearing surfaces do deteriorate so the bearings should be replaced at major rebuilds. Competition engines will need far more frequent bearing replacement because of the high valve spring pressures they use. The centre (there are usually only three camshaft bearings on inline four cylinder engines) camshaft bearing is subjected to more load than the bearings at each end and, as a consequence, wears quicker.

In block camshaft bearings wear in the direction of the loading which, in a conventional pushrod engine, is opposite the lifter and pushrod. Wear is usually clearly visible but, once again, direct measurement using an inside micrometer is the way to determine the true status of the bearing diameter. Bearing shell surface deterioration is another factor to consider.

If there is any doubt about camshaft bearings, replace them.

CONNECTING ROD BOLTS

Connecting rod bolts are made from high tensile steel and seldom fail in normal service. These bolts are highly stressed items and **must always** be replaced at major rebuilds. Connecting rod bolts can be crack tested but that only proves that at the time of the test the bolts were crack-free: shortly after being reinstalled in the engine these same bolts may develop cracks through fatigue and be the cause of a major engine failure. In any high-performance application the connecting rod bolts must be replaced with the best quality bolts available. Premium quality bolts are readily available for not too much more than

the price of factory original equipment bolts.

Caution! - When you replace stock bolts with new stock bolts (not recommended) or aftermarket high strength bolts, if the cap is located only by the shanks of the bolts, you **must** have the big end tunnels resized to restore their roundness.

Note that the lighter the piston and wrist pin combination, the lighter the forces acting on the two connecting rod bolts. The fitting of lightweight forged pistons and piston pins, as opposed to continuing to use the heavy standard piston and piston pin, is a good move to improve connecting rod reliability but, these days, pistons and piston pins are usually very light in standard form and not too much weight can be saved. Very modern standard pistons and pins are very light and this represents a significant change by automobile manufacturers: many of today's four cylinder in-line engines have the attributes of racing car engines.

GASKETS

The majority of gasket sets are of good quality, original equipment or otherwise. The only parts that may not be up to a high enough specification for high-performance applications are the cylinder head gaskets. Just about all four cylinder in-line head gaskets are of a composite type and will hold CRs of up to 11:1 in naturally aspirated (non super/turbocharged) engines. Most composite cylinder head gaskets last well on the standard engine but, with the application change, they may no longer be suitable. Original manufacturer cylinder head gaskets are generally better than aftermarket replacement cylinder head gaskets. For example, the standard Sierra Cosworth head

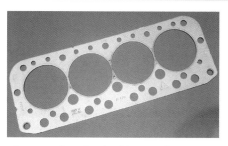

Inexpensive standard-type replacement composite cylinder head gasket. Will hold moderate compression (10.0:1) for a short period of time on any engine. Sometimes this is good enough for the application (lots of inexpensive head gaskets lots of times!)

Good quality standard factory cylinder head gasket. Will hold moderate compression (11:1) for a reasonable period of time.

Felpro 'Blue' cylinder head gasket which is Teflon coated and is advertised as being re-usable. Will hold high compression (12.0:1) with a cast iron block and cylinder head for a reasonable period of time.

gasket, made by Reinz, is excellent, and is considered the only gasket to use for competition or standard engines.

The blue Felpro cylinder head gasket, for example, is a rigid composite type gasket that is approximately 0.040in/1.0mm thick

Reinz-manufactured head gasket, which has a raised ridge ring seal around each bore, will hold high compression reliably for a long time.

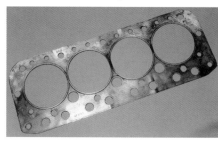

Copper/asbestos head gasket. Will hold high compression for a reasonable period of time provided the gasket matching surfaces are perfectly flat.

and, provided the cylinder head surface and the block deck surface are absolutely flat, these gaskets will not blow with CRs of up to 12:1. Obviously they will begin to leak at some stage, and it would be unreasonable to expect them not to, but, frequently, these gaskets last until the engine is stripped down for a regular rebuild. There are plenty of other good quality aftermarket high-performance cylinder head gaskets available that will hold higher than normal compression ratios.

Note: there is no substitute for perfectly flat block and head surfaces when it comes to good gasket sealing.

Freeze (Welch) plugs are made of plated steel or brass. All engines should use a rust inhibitor whether they are aluminium or not, and, with this in the water, the corrosion of the steel freeze plugs virtually ceases. All freeze plugs should be strapped to prevent them coming out, and all freeze plugs should be replaced at

each rebuild. This way the sealing between the plug and block is renewed regularly which helps to prevent potentially catastrophic water leakage.

O-RINGING BLOCKS

For engines that persistently blow head gaskets the solution is to O-ring the block. This entails machining a groove in the deck surface around each cylinder and fitting copper wire into the groove so that the wire is proud of the block's deck by between 0.004-0.008in/0.10-0.20mm. If the gasket is a very rigid one like a Felpro, the wire's protrusion need be only 0.004in/0.10mm. If the gasket is a standard composite (thicker, less rigid and a more compressible) the amount of protrusion can be increased up to 0.008in/0.20mm.

If the diameter of the wire is 0.044in/1.10mm a square section groove is machined into the block that is 0.044in/1.10mm wide and 0.040in/1.0mm deep for 0.004in/0.10mm protrusion or 0.036in/0.90mm deep for 0.008in/0.20mm protrusion.

To establish the O-ring groove diameter, the cylinder head gasket bore and the the depth of the steel insert overlap are measured with a vernier caliper. The width of the steel insert is added to the as measured bore size of the gasket and this gives the diameter of the centre of the O-ring groove. The intention is that the wire contacts the gasket exactly in the centre of the steel insert (see accompanying picture).

To machine the groove the block is bolted on to the table of a turret-type milling machine (Bridgeport or similar), the centre of the bore found, the tool set for the right diameter and the groove cut to the right depth. This is has to be done very accurately by a competent operator. There are also tools available that locate into the bore and are rotated by hand to cut the groove (cast iron is relatively soft and this is quite possible) and these, too, can be made to give an accurate result.

The copper wire is carefully inserted into the groove and seated using a 'rawhide' headed hammer. The ends of the copper wire are filed by hand so that they are dead square. Initially one end is filed and inserted into the groove and then, when the circle is nearly completed, the other end of the wire is cut just over the final size then filed square to perfect length: there must be **no** overlap. It is a question of filing the end of the copper wire until, when it is finally and fully seated into the groove, there is virtually no gap to be seen. This process takes time and a few bits of copper wire may be ruined in the process but persistence will be rewarded by near absolute cylinder head gasket reliability.

With the block treated like this the gaskets will be as compression tight as practicably possible. It's still possible to blow a gasket but it seldom happens. Very high compressions and working pressures can be maintained with O-ringed blocks so the method is strongly recommended if absolute reliability is required.

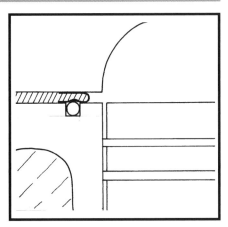

O-ring must be positioned so that it contacts the gasket halfway across the width of the gasket's steel insert.

Chapter 4
Plain bearing basics

Crankshaft main bearings and the connecting rod big end bearings require careful fitting and the correct clearances if the bottom end of an engine is to give good service. Simply fitting the bearing shells to the block and main caps, installing the crankshaft, fitting the main caps and torquing the bolts is **not** acceptable practice for a high-performance engine. That method of fitting bearings may well be the way the majority of rebuilt stock engines are assembled, but when this technique is applied to high-performance engines the failure rate escalates dramatically.

BEARING TUNNELS

The principle of all shell type bearing (mains & con rods) fitting relies on the fact that the tunnel in which the bearing shells are held is 100% round, the correct size and has a good surface finish. If the tunnel does not meet these criteria the engine is flawed from

View shows the block tunnel diameter that is formed when the main cap is fitted to the block and the bolts correctly torqued.

here on.

The tunnel bore diameter of main and big end bearings - measured with the caps fitted and retaining bolts correctly torqued - **must** be parallel across its width. This is reasonably easy to measure with an inside micrometer by taking three measurements across the width of the tunnel (see photos). Connecting rod tunnels are much the same in width as main bearing tunnels. If the tunnel bore proves to be not parallel, the

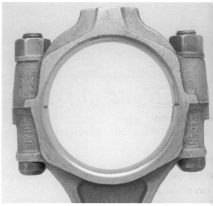

View shows the connecting rod tunnel diameter that is formed when the connecting rod cap is fitted to the connecting rod and the bolts correctly torqued.

tunnel is **not** suitable for further service and, in the case of a mains, they will have to be align-bored while connecting rods will have to have their bearing bores resized.

The main bearing and connecting rod bearing tunnel surfaces **must** be absolutely clean as **must** the main cap

Check parallelism of main bearing tunnels. Measure with an inside micrometer in the centre of the tunnel and as near to both edges as possible (about 0.125in/3mm in is about as close to the edges as is practicable).

Check parallelism of connecting rod big end tunnels by measuring at three points through the tunnels width.

registers of the block, the bases of the main cap and the partline faces of the con rods: any dirt or metal particles that remain could cause measuring and fitting to be incorrect. Clean the block and cap surfaces with paper towels and use a solvent such as paint thinner to remove all traces of dirt and grime.

BEARING SHELL LOCATION TABS

All bearing shells are located (for positioning purposes only) by tabs. The tab is part of the bearing shell and is pressed away from the bearing

Bearing shell showing the tab which will locate the bearing shell in the tunnel. This bearing shell is also grooved.

shell's internal diameter. All main bearing and connecting rod bearing shells use this system.

Connecting rod bearing shells will frequently interchange, even though one bearing shell of the pair may have a small hole in it for thrust face piston skirt oiling. Squirting oil on to the bore wall in this manner has now largely been discontinued as there is a tendency for too much oil to be put on the bore walls and this overloads the oil control rings.

The main bearing shells will have the tabs in different positions. For instance the block bearing shell may have the tabs to one side of the bearing shell while the cap bearing shells may have central tabs. Location tabs in no way contribute to the prevention of 'bearing spin.'

FITTING MAIN BEARING SHELLS

The tabs of the bearing shells fit into either the block or main cap. The tabs are in different positions on block bearing shells when compared to cap bearing shells but, for quick reference, the grooved bearings fit in the block. The width of most shell bearing inserts ranges between 0.775in and 0.925in/ 19.6mm and 23.5mm.

The new bearing shells must be

Bearing shell location notch in the block tunnel as machined by the factory. Make sure that all location notches are thoroughly clean.

Bearing shell sitting in the tunnel of a block. The tab on the bearing shell and the notch machined in the block are in line and will locate the bearing shell correctly. At this point the bearing shell has not been pressed (by hand) fully into the tunnel. Note that the end of the bearing shell and tab are 0.375in/4.5mm down from the register surface.

thoroughly cleaned so that when they are installed the contact between the bearing shell and the block is as close to metal-to-metal as possible. Clean the bearing shells using paper towels and a solvent such as paint thinner. Absolute cleanliness is **vital** for successful bearing fitting.

The bearing shell is placed into the tunnel with the tab located in the machined notch of the block. The side of the bearing shell that has the tab is first located 0.187in/4.5mm below the part line of the tunnel. The other end of the bearing shell will stick up above the part line of the tunnel until the shell is pressed down (by hand) into

Main bearing shell about to be pressed by hand into the block tunnel.

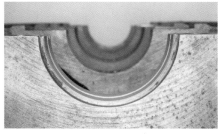

Ends of the bearing shell insert when correctly fitted to the tunnel.

Main bearing shell is pressed down until opposite end comes up flush with the surface of the main bearing cap.

Main bearing shell fully installed in the main cap. Ends of the bearing shell are level.

the tunnel. The action for pressing the bearing shell into the tunnel involves downward pressure as well as slight inward pressure.

Both ends of all bearing shell inserts must end up at equal heights in relation to the part line of the block or cap. This usually means that the ends of the bearing shell inserts appear to be level with the matching surface or slightly above. If the ends of the bearing shell inserts are found to be slightly below the level of the matching surface of the block that, too, can be acceptable, but expect the ends of the bearing shell insert that is fitted to the matching cap to be prouder of the part line than usual. The bottom line of fitting bearing shell inserts is that there must be sufficient bearing 'crush' (the outside diameter of the bearing is slightly larger than the tunnel inside diameter).

The main cap bearing shell is a plain bearing without a groove. To install the bearing shells in the caps hold the cap in a vice fitted with jaw covers so that the caps will not be marked by the jaw serrations.

Note that combination main bearing/thrust shell inserts are usually more difficult to fit and seat into the block and cap than the other bearing shells. More than hand force is usually

Bearing shell positioned in the cap ready to be pressed down into the tunnel. The end of the bearing shell is 0.375/4.5mm below the surface of the cap.

necessary and the bearing shell can be assisted into position with a 1in diameter plastic rod. The rod can be tapped very lightly with a hammer. The softness of the plastic will ensure that the bearing shell is not damaged. Position the bearing shell by hand as much as possible in the first instance.

With the bearing shells fitted to the block tunnel and to the main bearing cap, the cap is placed into the block register (no crankshaft). The cap will not be a hand fit into the block register due to the cap being an interference fit into the block. In the first instance, the cap is fitted into the register with one side of the cap up on the edge of the block register and it is then tapped into its register using a copper or plastic hammer.

FITTING BIG END BEARINGS

Connecting rod bearing shells are fitted in the same manner as main

Bearing shell correctly fitted. The tab of the shell is located in the notch and the bearing shell has been pressed into the tunnel until the ends of the bearing shell are level.

Bearing shell being pressed by hand into the cap. The bearing shell receives downward pressure.

A 1in/25mm diameter plastic rod being used to position this combination thrust/main bearing shell. Tapping lightly with a small hammer on the rod is all that's necessary to move the bearing shell. Note that the plastic rod is square on to the end of the bearing shell.

Cap being 'snapped' into position using a copper hammer lightly.

Bearing shell being pressed into position by hand.

Bearing shell correctly positioned in a connecting rod. The ends of the bearing shell level.

Cap sitting in the block register with one side of the cap up on the edge of the block register ready to be "snapped" into position.

The completed bearing assembly. The bolts are correctly torqued.

Bearing shell positioned on the cap. The tab is located in the notch before the shell is pushed into position.

bearing shells. It's helpful if the connecting rod or cap is held firmly in a vice (protective shields fitted) but installation of the bearing shell can be quite successfully carried out with the connecting rod or cap hand held.

The bearing shell is seated into the connecting rod by applying downward pressure with two fingers to that part of the bearing shell that is proud of the tunnel. Fitting of the bearing shell in this manner ensures that the shell is seated into the tunnel without any scraping of the back surface.

The connecting rod cap can be

Bearing shell placed into the tunnel of a connecting rod. The tab end of the bearing shell is 0.125in/3mm down from the partline surface.

easily held in a vice (with protective shields in place) and the bearing shell positioned in the tunnel so that the tab end of the bearing shell is 0.125in/3mm down from the partline of the cap.

The bearing shell is pressed down into the cap using thumb pressure.

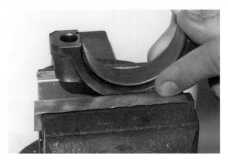

Bearing shell being pressed into the cap using moderate thumb pressure.

Bearing shell correctly positioned in a connecting rod cap.

The bearing shells are easier to fit if the tab end of the bearing shell is 0.125in/3mm down from the part line of the cap. The bearing shell simply slides into position and the ends of the bearing shell usually end up flush with the partline surfaces.

There are two forms of connecting rod cap fastening: 1) through bolt and nut (which has the shanks of the bolt locating the cap) and 2) the bolt that screws into the connecting rod and has the cap located by dowels, serrations, or similar. The former type is dealt with first.

With the bearing shells installed in both the connecting rod and cap, the cap is fitted onto the connecting rod bolts. The connecting rod bolts locate the cap and a degree of interference fit between the connecting rod bolts and cap is vital. The cap will become a tight fit when it is about 0.25in/6mm

Cap in position on the connecting rod bolts at the point where the holes of the cap and the bolt sizes are now a size for size fit.

Cap and connecting rod being drawn together using the nuts.

Connecting rod with the two bearings fitted and the nuts tensioned up just as the connecting rod will operate in service.

away from the connecting rod's matching face as the cap contacts the on-size diameter area of the bolts. This on-size diameter area will usually be in the form of knurling but some connecting rod bolt shanks are plain.

Bearing shell insert removal using the thumb and forward pressure.

The nuts are then wound down t where they contact the cap's spot facing. At this point the nuts are tensioned with a spanner and alternately wound down so that the connecting rod is effectively drawn to the cap with a reasonably equal gap constantly being maintained side to side. This way the cap and connecting rod are drawn to each other square on.

The nuts are used to draw the connecting rod and cap together by turning the nuts a half turn each alternately until the cap and connecting rod are together, and then tensioning the nuts to the recommended torque.

On a connecting rod using only bolts to retain the cap, the cap is removed by tapping the sides of the cap alternately with a copper hammer. With new bolts fitted this can be quite difficult, but the cap will always come off. The shell in the cap may become dislodged during this process. If the cap is a loose fit on the connecting ro bolts, with obvious cap movement present, the tunnel bore may not be round (0.001-0.002in/0.02mm-0.05mm out). **Caution** - the connecting rod is not suitable for further use in this condition. The cap **must** locate firmly onto the connecting rod bolts.

All bearing shells can be carefully removed and fitted as many times as is necessary during the check fitting procedure. Clean the bearing shells, tunnels and matching surfaces of the connecting rods and the block and main caps **every** time the bearing shells are refitted.

An easy method for removing bearing shell inserts is to apply moderate thumb pressure to the bearing shell. With thumb pressure pushing sideways the bearing shell insert simply flicks out of the tunnel bore. The exception to this is the combination type main bearing/thrust bearing which often requires a small screwdriver to be inserted into the location groove to prise the bearing shell insert away from the block and cap. Not too much force is required to do this.

Chapter 5
Cylinder block - checking

The success of your high performance rebuild relies on the block being 100% structurally sound. All engine parts are bolted/fixed to or contained by the block, so there can be no compromises with the engine block's overall strength. Basically the block must be damage and crack-free, be able to be rebored, have main caps that are tight in the block registers, have tunnel sizes that are mid-tolerance, or better, and have no damaged threaded holes.

Check the bore sizes as soon as the cylinder head has been removed because if the block has already been bored to the maximum the factory specify and is now well used, the block is useless unless there are further oversize pistons available (meaning that the particular engine block is known to be able to accept further boring). The ideal block is one that has standard but worn bores at the time of measuring; this will allow boring to the first overbore size.

A cylinder bore being measured with an inside micrometer. The very top of the bore will be 'on size' unless it has been machined with a ridge remover. The most worn part of the bore is going to be the top or, more specifically, about 0.375in/ 9mm down from the top. The base of the bore remains pretty much on size.

The problem with over-boring a block is that the bore walls become too thin and bore rigidity is **very important** for good piston ring sealing. The minimum over-bore size of most late model blocks is generally 0.020in/ 0.50mm. To increase the engine's capacity by excessive over-boring, which results in minimum thickness bore walls, seldom results in an increase in power while the reliability of the engine can be seriously reduced. The recommendation, unless it is positively known that the particular type of block concerned will take further boring than the factory recommends, is to stay within the factory range of oversizes. Boring to the maximum factory oversize instead of to the very next possible oversize to gain engine capacity (a few cc) is folly. Boring to the very next oversize is always the best option.

CHECKING MAIN BEARING TUNNEL SIZES

In the first instance the block's main bearing tunnel sizes (without bearings) are measured and then checked against the factory specifications to ascertain their status.

Note that main caps are **not** directly interchangeable from block to block. Blocks are originally line bored

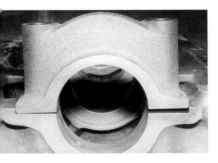

The main cap positioned on the block register but not yet 'snapped' into position.

A copper hammer is used to tap the cap into the register: light taps only are needed.

The main cap correctly fitted with its bolts correctly torqued.

A main bearing tunnel being measured in the vertical plane with an inside micrometer.

The main bearing tunnel being measured 60 degrees to the right of the vertical plane.

The main bearing tunnel being measured 60 degrees to the left of the vertical plane.

ith a set of caps fitted and after this machining process those caps will only uit that block. It is seldom possible for he main caps from another engine to e fitted and the tunnels to be the orrect size and fit (sheer luck if they re). Replacement caps can be fitted a block, but the block **must** then be ne-bored or align-honed to correct ny mismatch and to ensure accuracy.

The main caps are fitted into the lock, one at a time, starting from the ack or front of the engine. Each cap placed in its register and 'snapped' to place and the bolts fitted to the ap and torqued as per normal ssembly. The inside diameter of each unnel is measured with an inside icrometer in three planes. The first is the vertical plane, then 60 degrees the right and left of vertical. Record ll the measurements and match them gainst the factory listed sizes/

tolerances.

Engine machine shops have the relevant main bearing tunnel size - along with plus and minus tolerances - for your engine listed in a specification book they use: they are the ideal source of this essential information.

Tunnel sizes all have plus or minus tolerances. In referring to these sizes the factory listed size is called 'on size.' With the maximum tolerance added to this figure it is called the 'top size' and with the maximum tolerance subtracted it is called 'bottom size'.

Having a block with the main bearing tunnels at the correct size is a basic requirement for bottom end reliability. If these sizes are wrong (over sized) the engine build is flawed from this point onwards.

A problem with some poorly built engines is 'spun bearings' (the bearings have rotated in their tunnels). There is no great mystery about what causes this to happen: the problem is one of incorrect sizing and the relevant sizes could easily have been checked with accurate measurement. Despite this, tunnel sizes seldom seem to be measured and yet reliability of the bottom end of the engine depends on their being absolutely right.

The majority of engine blocks will be found to be 'on size' but, better

still, some will be on 'bottom size' (smallest diameter). Beware of blocks with tunnels that are on 'top size' (largest size).

Blocks with tunnels that are on 'top size' are likely to have a main bearing spin in them. The reason that blocks like this are prone to bearing spin is that the bearing shells have insufficient 'crush.' The bearings are held in the tunnel diameter but they do not necessarily conform to the tunnel shape as closely as they would

Main bearing tunnel which has been honed to size and has a very smooth cross hatched surface finish.

if they had more crush on them. The bearing shells are forced to conform perfectly to the shape of the tunnel when the amount of bearing crush is correct.

The reason most engine blocks are align-bored or align-honed is because the tunnel diameters are too large and not because the main bearing tunnel bores are not in line axially (as is sometimes thought).

If the blocks tunnel sizes are incorrect and the bearing shells prove to have insufficient bearing crush when they are check fitted, the block will have to be align-bored or align-honed to 'bottom size.' This work is carried out by an engine machine shop using align-honing or align-boring equipment.

Align-honing is used when up to 0.003in/0.075mm has to come out of the tunnels, while align-boring is used when more than 0.003in or 0.075mm has to come out of the tunnels.

The surface finish of block tunnels, if align bored, is similar to a lathe turned finish. This is quite different from the surface finish of the inside of a connecting rod tunnel which is honed. Align-honing, which does everything that align-boring does, gives a very smooth surface finish which is desirable. Many modern engines are finished this way as standard and, as a consequence, can

Main bearing tunnel which has been align-bored and has a surface finish the same as a lathe turned article.

be regarded as having an ideal tunnel finish.

CHECK FITTING MAIN BEARING SHELLS

The main bearing shells should be check fitted to find out if they have sufficient crush on them and to

Main bearings fitted to the front main of this block. Both bolts were installed and torqued to the correct setting.

Now one bolt has been removed (on the right hand side) which allows that side of the main bearing cap to spring up creating a gap which is then measured using a feeler gauge. The size of the gap denotes the amount of 'crush' that is holding the bearings in place.

measure the fitted inside diameter of the main bearings.

Checking bearing crush

With the block's tunnel sizes checked for size (minus bearing shells) and the block thoroughly cleaned, place each main bearing shell half into the block (but only immediately before the cap is going to be fitted). Check to make sure that the backs of the shells and the surface of the block's tunnel are perfectly clean. Install the main cap shells into the caps.

Start at the rear of the block and sit the cap into the block register and 'snap' the cap into place. Install the bolts and torque them as specified. Release the tension of one bolt by undoing it and the cap will spring up on that side. Check the size of the gap between the cap and the block register with a feeler gauge. Record the size of the gap, refit the bolt and retorque the bolt.

Expect to fit a feeler gauge with a thickness of between 0.003-0.005in/ 0.075-0.125mm. If a 0.001in/ 0.025mm gap is measured, this is not a sufficient amount of bearing crush and such a bearing could spin in service. If the gap between the block and cap measures 0.001in/0.025mm

...et the block tunnels were measured and found to be 'on size' or on bottom size,' the shells are not correct: replace the set of shells. The smaller the bearing diameter the smaller the crush height. So, as a general rule, consider 0.003in/0.075mm suitable for a 1000cc to 1400cc engine and 0.005in/0.125mm suitable for an 1800cc to 2000cc engine.

If the feeler gauge gap measurements vary between, say, 0.005in/0.125mm, 0.002in/0.05mm, 0.004in/0.10mm, 0.004in/0.10mm and 0.003in/0.075mm, swap the top shell from the cap of the main bearing with 0.005in/0.125mm with that of the main bearing with 0.002in/0.05mm. This procedure will tend to equalize, as far as possible, the bearing crush heights of all the pairs of shells.

When the main bearings spin, the shells form tightly around the crankshaft journal and, except for this, do not usually look very damaged. When the mains spin in their tunnels, oil is still being supplied to the backs of the main bearing shells. The backs of the bearing shells and the block tunnel surfaces will have some slight rotational score marks and the tabs of the shells will no longer be proud.

When a main bearing spins it cuts off the oil supply to one (or two, depending on engine design) connecting rod big end, which then overheats and destroys the connecting rod bearing. In this circumstance connecting rod bearings are always totally destroyed and look a mess. Frequently the assumption is made that the big end failed because the connecting rod bearing shows the most damage, but the real reason for the failure was a lack of sufficient bearing crush on the main bearings.

If the bearing crush is insufficient (0.001in/0.025mm, or less) because

The cap being measured with an outside micrometer. This is done, on each side of the cap, before any material is removed. Material removal relative to the original measurement is monitored by frequent remeasurement.

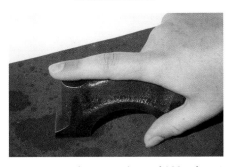

Main cap resting on a sheet of 220 grit wet and dry paper which, in turn, is resting on a perfectly flat surface. The cap is moved back and forth with firm hand pressure which also holds the cap in full contact with the flat surface: this serves to ensure that a uniform amount of material is removed from the cap surface.

the bearing tunnels are on 'top size,' the caps can have a small amount of material removed from their mating surfaces. The maximum amount of material that can be removed from a cap's mating surface is 0.002in/0.05mm. This is an acceptable method of restoring bearing crush within a very narrow range.

This restoration of crush can be achieved by placing a new sheet of 220 grit, wet and dry paper face up on to a **perfectly** flat surface (engineers surface plate, or a thick plate glass panel) and, with the bearing shell removed, moving the cap back and

forth until a small amount of material is removed from the base of the cap (the actual amount of material to remove being governed by the increase in bearing crush required).

The modified cap is cleaned, has the bearing shell fitted and is then refitted to the engine block and the crush height measured again. When the crush is acceptable, stop removing material from the cap mating surface. **Caution! - Do not** remove more than 0.002in/0.05mm from the cap as the bearing tunnel will become out of round.

Measuring main bearing inside diameters

The inside diameter sizes of individual main bearings can be used by the engine reconditioner to regrind the crankshaft so that every individual bearing has exactly the same running clearance when assembled. This will mean that individual journals are ground to a specific size (within the plus and minus tolerance). The crankshaft journal diameters may well all end up the same size, but they might also all be slightly different (but all within the factory tolerance) to one another: this is acceptable in an effort to gain optimum bearing clearances. It is far more correct and desirable to end up with all bearings having the same running clearance with some individual crankshaft journals slightly larger or smaller, than it is to have all journals ground to the same size and have varying bearing clearances which may mean that some bearings are tight.

(Note that it is usual for all subsequent replacement bearing sets to fit into the block in a similar manner to the new bearings that are being check fitted now: but **always** check fit each new set to be sure).

Having established correct

An inside micrometer being used to measure the inside diameter of a main bearing bore in the vertical plane.

Inside micrometer being used to measure the inside diameter of a main bearing bore 60 degrees to the right of vertical.

Inside micrometer being used to measure the inside diameter of a main bearing bore 60 degrees to the left of vertical.

bearing crush heights, fit the main bearing caps (with both block and cap bearings in place, but no crankshaft) and torque their retaining bolts to manufacturer's specification. Using an inside micrometer, check the inside diameter of each main bearing in three places (see photos). The desired bearing running clearance is

subtracted from the inside diameter of each bearing which then gives you the actual crankshaft journal size needed for each bearing. Record the information.

Caution! - Never put new bearings into a block and hope for the best. Always check fit all bearing sets for crush and then measure the inside

diameter bores of the main bearings and compare them against the crankshaft journal diameter to make sure that the prescribed running clearance is present. To run an engine which has insufficient bearing crush, insufficient bearing clearance or too much bearing clearance is asking for trouble.

Chapter 6
Cylinder block
- preparation

When the initial checks that prove the cylinder block is suitable for rebuilding have been completed, the block can be thoroughly cleaned, remachined and generally prepared for assembly.

CLEANING COMPONENTS

Cast iron components

The block must be thoroughly cleaned back to bare metal; this is best done by an engine machine shop which will use a cleaning tank commonly called a 'Hot Tank.' This type of tank is used to clean all cast iron and steel parts such as crankshafts and connecting rods. **Caution!** - the hot tank cleaning process **does not** remove all dirt and grime, but most of it. The parts that come out of the cleaning tank will still need to be detailed by hand to ensure 100% cleanliness.

Hot tanks vary in size, but usually they can take two or three blocks at a time. These tanks contain a water-based caustic soda solution, which is an alkalide mix, heated to between 60 and 90 degrees C/140 and 194 degrees F (the hotter the better generally). Parts can be left soaking overnight.

Aluminium components

Aluminium components are cleaned in a tank that contains an undiluted solution of cresylic acid and methylene chloride that is used cold. The parts to be cleaned are immersed in the fluid and left for a minimum of one hour, but can be left in the tank overnight, if necessary, without detriment to the aluminium. Parts come out of the tank with a matt finish.

Most tanks are large enough to take an aluminium cylinder block, but no more, because of the expense involved in filling the tank with the solution. The tank will also have a boundary layer of water on top of the solution (about 4in/100mm deep) to prevent evaporation.

Preparation before cleaning

Before the parts are taken to the engine machine shop remove all screw in oil gallery plugs, press in plugs, freeze plugs, wet liners (if applicable) and the camshaft bearings (if applicable). Be **absolutely thorough** with the cleaning of the engine block: it only takes a few dirt particles to become dislodged and get into the oiling system to cause a serious bearing failure.

If the camshaft is situated in the block and the bearings are new and it is decided to leave them in place, the bearing surfaces will be damaged beyond further use if the cleaning solution is allowed to come into contact with them. The only way to prevent the bearings from getting damaged is to leave the camshaft in place when the block is placed in the hot tank.

The main caps, conrods and crankshaft should also be taken to the engine machine shop and put in the hot tank for cleaning. Have the pistons pressed off the connecting rods (if they are of this type) by the engine machine shop before the conrods are put in the hot tank as there is no point in cleaning parts that are going to be discarded.

Cleaning after parts have been in the tank

All oil galleries must be scraped clean using long mild steel rods and then wiped clean inside so that they are like new. The latter can be achieved by hacksawing a slot in the end of a suitable rod and using this slot to trap the end of a small piece of clean rag so that the rod can be rotated by hand as it is fed into the oil gallery. The piece of rag cannot be too large as it will tend to jam in the hole and can then be very difficult to remove. Change the piece of rag frequently until the rag comes out of the oil gallery clean.

Note that most blocks have screw-in plugs at the ends of the oil galleries but some blocks have a press-in plug or ball at the one end -

A long mild steel rod with a slot hacksawed in the end, a small piece of rag trapped in the slot and the rag wound around the rod, is used to scrape the oil galleries. The rod is fed into the block while it is being rotated by hand. The rag will not unwind and jam provided the rod is rotated one way only (the way it was wound on).

especially on the main longitudinal oil gallery.

It is acceptable to leave a pressed-in plug or ball in position and use a long rod to clean right up to the back of it. In many instances, for ultimate reliability, press-in plugs/balls are removed and the hole tapped to take a threaded plug. Another possible solution is to stake the plug in position (many engine manufacturers do this from new).

Spray-can engine degreasers can be used successfully to clean off, or loosen, any remaining dirt on the block surfaces. Block surfaces can be rotary wire brushed and hand scraped to remove the most stubborn grime build ups.

The waterways in the block must be checked to ensure that there is absolutely no solid build-up of limescale/sediment anywhere. Even if the block has been thoroughly cleaned in the hot tank, always check the waterways just to make sure there is nothing there. Use 0.125in/3mm to 0.375in/4mm diameter steel rods as probes to get into the waterways through the freeze plug holes and the waterway outlets in the block deck.

Scrape around everywhere in the waterways and use compressed air to blow the dirt particles out (**Warning!** - always use eye protection when using compressed air). The rods can be used to gauge the depth of the waterways so that if the rods do not go right down to the bottom of the waterway there is a fair chance that there is very hard sediment present. If sediment is not cleaned away, it can lead to engine overheating. The waterways around the rearmost cylinders are the worst offenders (in north-south-engined cars) as the sediment goes to the back of the block because engines are invariably angled down at the back when in place in the car.

Press in oil gallery plug (left) and screw i (right).

Pressed in oil gallery plug in place.

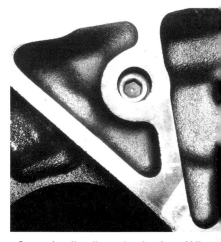

Screw in oil gallery plug in place (Allen-headed).

Ball pressed into the end main oil gallery ('Pinto' block).

CRACK & POROSITY TESTING

Iron blocks

After thorough cleaning, in the first instance visually check the outside surfaces of the block, bores, crankcase and the lifter chamber/s for obvious cracks. Cracks are usually very visible and a magnifying glass can be used with good effect to track them down. All traces of paint must be removed so that the metal surface can be thoroughly checked.

With the block and main bearing caps thoroughly cleaned they can be crack tested. In the case of the cast-iron block and caps, these are temporarily magnetized and a solution of Magnaflux powder and paraffin (kerosene) is sprayed over the block and caps: where there is a crack, the metal filings in the powder congregate and this will be clearly seen when viewed with a 'black light.'

On wet liner blocks, thoroughly inspect the registers in which the liners sit and the surrounding area from both the crankshaft and liner sides. The main bearing webs and the block structure in this area are very highly loaded.

After the crack testing the block and main caps are demagnetized. The skill of the operator using the crack testing equipment plays a huge part in the detection of cracks. Part of this skill is knowing where to look in the block structure.

When cylinders are bored out to 0.060in/1.5mm the bores can become porous. This doesn't happen very often but, if it does, the block is a write-off for high-performance use as the block has to be sleeved to fix the problem. Cracks are visible when a cylinder is actually being rebored, looking like a faint to heavy black line depending on how bad the crack is).

Porosity, on the other hand, usually shows up as a non-uniform surface with what appear to be black dots on an otherwise freshly machined, shiny surface. A skilled machinist will usually notice a crack or porosity when machining the bore.

If a block is suspected of being porous, the block should be pressure tested. Not all imperfections that look like porosity are, in fact, porous. To check the block all water outlets are blocked off and hot water is circulated through the block, then the water is subjected to at least 50psi/344kpa of air pressure (engine machine shops have equipment to check this). If the bore wall is porous, water will seep through and form a wet area or a drip. If there is a hole, water will come out in a fine stream. If nothing happens the block will not leak in service, even though the surface imperfections are present.

If a crack or cracks are found around the bores, head stud holes, main bearings or any other structural area by the crack testing procedure, the block will have to be scrapped - **bad parts are worse than no parts**. Source alternative parts if there is any doubt as to the integrity of the parts you have.

Aluminium blocks

After they have been thoroughly cleaned, aluminium blocks are initially checked all over for cracks visually. Use a magnifying glass to look for cracks and damaged areas. Look for damage on the top of the block around the cylinder head gasket line where, if the head gasket has blown and the engine has been run for any length of time in this condition, there could be a major problem. Such blocks can require welding and remachining to restore the surface so that it is serviceable. If any suspect

areas are found, ring them with chalk for more thorough checking. Narrow down any problem areas so that they can be concentrated on. While most cracks in aluminium blocks tend to be quite easy to see, once located they should be thoroughly investigated to prove whether they are true cracks or not.

Aluminium wet liner blocks are, by design, very rigid structures as the liners are not a structural part of the block: the lower part of such a block has to support liners and crankshaft. Because the structural integrity of wet liner blocks is so essential, only completely sound blocks are suitable for high performance use.

The next step is to use a dye penetrant on the problem areas you have located. Kits consist of three spray cans and can be used on ferrous and non-ferrous materials (that is cast iron, steel, aluminium, brass, and so on). **Warning!** - these chemicals can be dangerous, so read the directions on each can to avoid problems. The first spray-can is a cleaner/solvent which removes all traces of dirt and grime from the surface. The second spray-can contains a penetrant which will get into any crack. The third spray-can contains a developer (fluorescent pink/purple in colour) and when this is sprayed on to the surface it highlights cracks by forming a solid line of a deep purple colour in or on the crack. There is no mistaking the colour change on the crack. If there is no crack, no line will be formed and the colour of the developer will dry uniform light pink.

These crack testing kits are readily available from specialist automotive suppliers and can be used by anyone, with excellent results if due care is taken.

If a crack or cracks are found by the crack testing procedure around the bores, head stud holes, main bearings or any other structural area, the block will have to be scrapped - **bad parts are worse than no parts**. Source alternative parts if there is any doubt as to the integrity of the parts you have.

THREADED HOLES

Clean out all threaded holes **thoroughly** by first using a probe or scriber to remove any dirt and particles from the bottom of the hole. Studs and bolts can be installed in holes which are not clear with disastrous results (cracking occurs). Use a solvent to wash the threads out and dissolve any oil and grease that maybe in the thread. Blow each hole out with compressed air and continue to clean out each hole individually until the threads are 100% clean and clear and back to shiny metal. **Warning!** - use eye protection whenever compressed air is being used.

Check each threaded hole by running a stud or bolt (that has had its thread well cleaned and wire brushed and has no damage of any description on the thread) into it. Avoid using taps in aluminium blocks if at all possible because they tend to remove material. Any stud or bolt should be able to be wound into the threaded hole easily by hand. Check the thread of the stud or bolt for grime/dirt particles when it is removed and wash the thread in the block and stud or bolt again, if necessary.

Check the surface around all threaded holes for 'pulling up' which indicates a damaged thread. Damaged threads can be repaired quite successfully with Helicoils. Good threads look good and sharp without any burring. Suspect threads almost

always show signs of galling or have shiny rub markings on them. Take absolute care with threaded holes in aluminium as it is not a very forgiving material.

Caution! - Do not be tempted to use studs or bolts that have shorter threaded portions than the originals on threaded holes in blocks which must take full tightening torque such as cylinder head bolts or main cap bolts: aluminium blocks always require maximum thread contact. Check to make sure that the right bolts or studs go into the right holes and make sure that no bolt 'bottoms out' as a bolt with this problem will not be effecting full clamping pressure.

Summary

At this point the block is thoroughly cleaned back to bare metal.
The block casting and main caps are proven to be crack-free.
The fit of the main caps in their block registers (or other locating devices) is correct.
The main bearing tunnel sizes have been checked and all are within tolerance.
The main bearings have the correct crush height.

At this point the block is definitely the one that is going to be used in the final build. However, there are several additions to the block (detailed in the following sections of this chapter) that are desirable as insurance against possible failure and convenience of maintenance. The time to carry out these extra operations is now because, after boring and honing, the block will be cleaned again in a tank for a final time. This is to give the machined surfaces a thorough clean and remove any particles of metal that will have found their way into the passageways, holes and other nooks and crannies of the block.

DRAIN TAP

If not already fitted, a drain tap is necessary to facilitate the removal of the coolant from the cylinder block. When the cylinder head is removed, for example, it is essential that no water is able to get into the bore. Some engine installations do not allow for easy access to the bottom radiator hose to allow coolant to be drained until its level is below the cylinder head gasket line. Admittedly water can be removed from the bore but it is preferable not to allow water to get in there in the first place.

Drain tap fitted to a block.

Place the drain tap as low in the block as you can, so that as much water as possible can be drained. Most engine blocks have casting bosses which can be utilised as drain plug sites. If there is no boss on the block, a suitable hole can be drilled into the waterway in the side of the block in a thickened or ribbed area: **Caution!** - the material thickness needs to be at least 0.312in/8mm so that good thread depth is available for a screw-in drain plug. The block can be drilled and tapped for a 1/4 BSP or 1/4 NPT hexagon-headed pipe plug. **Caution!**

Use plumbers' thread tape on any drain plug.

STRAPPING WELCH (FREEZE) & CAMSHAFT PLUGS

In service Welch plugs do not come out of blocks all that frequently but, when they do, all of the coolant is lost in an instant and the engine is usually severely damaged: positive retention is the only way to avoid this happening. If the plug comes loose (even though strapped) the water will leak out much more slowly and rising temperature will give some warning before the engine is overheated.

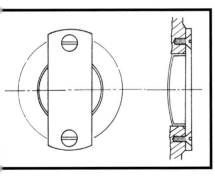

A sectioned side view of the block, freeze plug and strap. Use a sealant on the fastening screw threads.

Straps are made from 0.125in/3mm thick by 1in/25mm wide aluminium flat bar. The aluminium is marked out and drilled so that the threads in the block are in a thick area and not near the edge of the freeze plug hole.

Use silicone sealer on all plugs: smear sealer on the block recess then wipe off the excess sealer after fitting the plug. The camshaft plug (if applicable) in the back of the block must be strapped as well because, if it comes out, oil will leak out very fast with disastrous results.

BLOCK DECKING

The block deck of a dry linered cast iron or alloy block **must** be flat for perfect cylinder head gasket sealing. Always remachine the top of the block when the engine is being rebuilt because it removes all possible doubt about the block, especially if head gasket problems arise later. Plane the block's deck before cylinder boring so that the bores' top chamfers can be put back on using the cylinder boring head after the cylinders have been rebored.

Note that the liners of a wet liner block stand proud of the block deck so that when the head is tightened down, the liners are forced onto their seats. **Caution!** - Ensure that wet liners protrude by an amount which is within the engine manufacturer's tolerance.

The decks of wet liner blocks can be planed to restore the surface, but the liners **must** also be machined to ensure that their protrusion stays within specification.

Before remachining the block deck there are some other

A piston being measured from crown down to the underside of piston pin. Measuring accuracy to within 0.002in/0.05mm is acceptable.

considerations.

When the engine was first stripped down, the distance from the block deck to the piston crown at TDC (top dead centre) was recorded for future reference. If the piston crown is 0.020in/0.50mm to 0.030in/0.75mm down the bore at TDC and engine compression is going to be increased, the very best way to achieve a higher CR (compression ratio) is to plane the block deck by a suitable amount. There are limits as to how much the deck can be planed but, until the pistons are brought up flush with the top of the block, this is an excellent way of increasing compression.

To calculate how much material can be removed, an original and one of the new pistons will have to be measured from the crown to the top of the wrist pin. If the measurements are the same, the distance the crown is down the bore at TDC will remain the same. These measurements will usually be identical through a set of pistons.

If, for example, the original piston crown was 0.030in/0.75mm down the bore and the new piston is 0.010in/0.25mm less in height from crown to wrist pin, it will take 0.040in/1.0mm of block planing to bring the pistons up flush with the top of the block. Note that too much compression will cause pre-ignition, so the required compression ratio needs to have been decided upon before planing.

Further to this, some engines have very thick cylinder head gaskets (up to 1.75mm/0.065in compressed) and in such cases the block can be machined so that the piston is proud of the block, but not more than 0.025in/0.6mm. **Caution!** - The top of the piston and the cylinder head surface should always have a minimum of 0.040in/1.0mm clearance at TDC. This allows for reasonable carbon build-up and rod stretch. Bringing the pistons up flush with the top of the block is safe, while planing the block so that the piston crowns are proud of the block can lead to problems with the piston crowns hitting the cylinder head if a thinner cylinder head gasket is ever fitted.

Normally when the block's deck is remachined to clean it up, about 0.003in/0.075mm to 0.005in/0.125mm will be removed. However, it's a relatively simple thing to keep on grinding and to remove up to 0.030in/0.75mm, or so. This will cost more than a normal skim, but it is still a good value for money way to gain compression.

To ensure that the block deck surface is absolutely flat, ask the machinist to take a series of small depth finishing cuts and allow the machine to 'spark out' before removing the wheel head from the work. This is nothing more than making sure that no sparks and therefore metal are still coming off the surface of the block as the wheel is passed across the work. When the sparks stop, the deck is flat. Small depth finishing cuts will remove any humps and hollows that may have resulted from taking large cuts.

Note that block decks are not always parallel with the crankshaft axis. Most blocks are on average within 0.001in/0.005in or 0.02mm/0.12mm end for end. The ultimate result of block deck error is that the distance down from the block deck to the top of the pistons at top dead centre will vary. Block deck error over about 0.004in/0.10mm should be corrected when remachining the block deck. The main criteria is that the block's deck surface is absolutely flat to preclude cylinder head gasket failure: the variation in the distance from the centre of the crankshaft

Where the piston skirt is measured.

tunnels to the block's deck, end for end, can cause a compression difference from front to back, but not much.

The only way to accurately measure block height and deck parallelism is with a large outside micrometer. Most engine machine shops (engine reconditioners) have these large outside micrometers and can measure a block to within 0.001in/0.02mm. The front of most engine blocks is reasonably easy to measure, but the rear of most blocks can cause some problems because the rear main is not at the edge of the block and the oil seal recess gets in the way. Engine machine shops can machine block decks to within 0.001in/0.02mm.

REBORING

Before the block is rebored, the piston diameters must all be measured at the base of the skirt and the size of each piston - to four digits (3.3870in/86.00mm for example) - written on the piston crown using a felt-tipped pen. The required clearance is added to the individual piston diameter and this becomes the size to which the relevant cylinder is bored and honed.

Optimum clearance for cast pistons for high performance use is the engine manufacturer's recommended maximum tolerance. Forged pistons require more clearance than cast ones,

Piston and connecting rod side on, showing (arrowed) the numbers on the top of the piston and the partline of the connecting rod.

so be guided by the piston manufacturer's recommendation - even if the suggested clearance seems very large.

Frequently the pistons will all be

A piston in its bore with the arrow on its crown facing the front of the engine. The matching piston number is clearly visible near the side of the block.

piston side on. The piston pin is clearly seen to be offset to the left.

entical in size (to the last digit) but, if ey are not, it's exceedingly unlikely at the pistons will vary by any more an 0.0002in/0.005mm within a set. all of the pistons within a set are ithin 0.0002in/0.005mm, that set n, for all intents and purposes, be onsidered to have pistons that are entical in size.

The cylinders are bored to suit the rgest piston. If 0.0025in/0.065mm is e desired piston to bore clearance nd all cylinders are bored and honed the same size, the smallest piston ill have a piston to bore clearance of 0027in/0.07mm which is entirely cceptable. It is always more likely that piston will be undersize (below the ted or nominal size) rather than versized within a set.

If the pistons vary in size by more an 0.0002in/0.006mm they will efinitely have to be allocated to a articular cylinder and numbered ccordingly. Each piston **must** have e correct piston to bore clearance ithin tolerance.

Irrespective of the size of the dividual pistons, it's good engine uilding practice to number the pistons a particular bore. The crown of the ston is engraved (avoid stamping)

with the appropriate number so that the number on the piston and the numbers at the connecting rod part-line are on the same side when piston and connecting rod are assembled. This way there will be no mistakes as to piston orientation and no possibility of ending up with cylinders that have the wrong pistons in them.

Most pistons have an arrow on the crown to indicate the forward facing position of the piston. This means that when the pistons are installed in the engine, all of the arrows will be facing towards the front of the engine so that the piston pin offset is the right way round.

Note that pistons have offset piston pins to reduce piston noise or 'piston slap.'

On a clockwise rotating engine, the wrist pin is positioned nearest the side of the piston that actually takes the thrust action. Looking at the engine from the front, a piston's thrust face is the one nearest the left-hand side of the block.

Cylinder block boring machines

Most engine machine shops will bore the block on an overhead boring machine which will have the block clamped to the machine base, or table, but without main caps fitted and torqued or a head plate fitted to simulate a fitted cylinder head. Some machine shops may have head boring plates to suit the particular engine to be bored and will use them on request. Note that aluminium blocks require careful handling to avoid damage to the surfaces.

The older type of reboring machine clamps on to the top of the block itself. Blocks machined with these machines rely on the fact that the top of the block is parallel with the crankshaft axis. When reconditioning a

block the deck is remachined to ensure that it is dead flat and, if this type of boring bar is to be used, the machinist will always measure the block to check it and make the necessary allowance so that the block's deck is perfectly parallel with the crankshaft axis. Boring blocks out with this type of machine gives accurate results, with good operators.

With the older type of boring machine, the machinist will line up the boring bar with the original bore by locating the centre of the bore using the unworn bottom part of the bore. A 'scratch cut' will be taken to check alignment against the original bore (excluding wear) and then a full cut taken.

For absolute accuracy of cylinder boring the block must be located by the main bearing bores, have the main caps fitted with their bolts correctly torqued and a head simulating plate and a head gasket fitted to the top of

Outer block rail edge being filed to remove the sharp edge formed when it was machined.

Inner edge of a block rail being filed to remove sharp edge.

Main bearing register being filed to remove the sharp edge, using a needle file.

Completed main bearing register which has had all sharp edges chamfered (0.004in/0.10mm).

The edge of the block deck being hand filed to remove the sharp edge formed during planing. The removal of sharp edges (that do not need to be sharp) is good engineering practice and reduces the possibility of personal injury.

the block. This method allows the block to be bored under the stress conditions it will have when assembled. Main caps can be fitted when either type of boring machine is used.

All rebored cylinders should be power honed to the surface finish required. Machines are specifically designed to do this job, and cannot really be bettered, but a good operator can finish the bores correctly by hand.

FINAL BLOCK DETAILING

After the block has been bored and honed, remove all sharp edges using hand files, rotary files and, perhaps, scrapers before the block is placed in the cleaning tank for the last time for a final cleaning to remove all dust and particles from the boring and decking processes. Note that the top of each bore should be chamfered by the

machinist when the block is rebored, though, if necessary, an appropriate chamfer can be filed.

Dry the block using compressed air and blow every passageway clear. **Warning!** - wear eye protection when using compressed air.

INSTALL CAMSHAFT BEARINGS (IF APPLICABLE)

At this point, if the block is of camshaft in block type, the camshaft bearings can now be installed. Most engine machine shops use an adjustable tool that can install camshaft bearings in virtually any engine. Get the engine machine shop to install the camshaft bearings, but **do** check that the oil holes in each bearing line up with the block's oilways and that the front bearing is recessed slightly from the block's machined surface (0.002-0.005in/0.05-0.125mm) **before** the

block is taken away from the engine machine shop. Also install the camshaft to be used into the block and check it for ease of rotation: if there is any binding, the time to find out about it and sort it out is now.

MACHINED SURFACE PROTECTION

With the machining work completed and the block now ready for assembly coat all machined surfaces with a spray-on oil such as WD-40 or CRC type lubricants to prevent surface rust forming on them. Always keep the block fully covered - a large plastic bag is ideal - from now on, except for when it is being worked on.

Chapter 7
Connecting rods
- preparation

Virtually all the standard connecting rods found in modern four cylinder engines, of any capacity, are capable of staying in one piece up to 6500rpm. Many standard connecting rods are capable of much more than this - with reliability. Small engines (up to1200cc) connecting rods are relatively safe to 7500-8000rpm, those of 1400cc-1600cc engines to 7000-7500rpm and those of 2000cc+ engines to 6500-7000rpm.

Caution! - The term "relatively safe" is used here on the basis that there can be **no absolute guarantee** with standard production connecting rods: there is always going to be the odd failure, so some risk is attached to their use in high-performance applications. New standard connecting rods are always a safer bet than used standard connecting rods.

Many standard connecting rods look quite thin and flimsy, yet they do not break even at 8000rpm. The reason for this is that the associated pistons are quite light (small bore engine). The Austin Rover 1275cc A-series engine, for example, has long connecting rods which do not look all that strong, yet many drivers turn these engines to 8000 to 8500rpm on a regular basis in competition events and failures are few and far between.

Most modern 2000cc engines' standard connecting rods will stand 7000rpm and 7500rpm if heavy duty connecting rod bolts are fitted. If higher rpm than this is required, then aftermarket connecting rods (Arrow, Carillo and Farndon, to name a few) will have to be used and will allow maximum rpm to be increased to 9000 plus. These special heavy duty connecting rods are the best type available and failures are few and far between (even at 9000 to 10000rpm) - but take note that any connecting rod can fail: there are limits to the durability of all components.

Many engines have heavy duty/high-performance relatives built by the same manufacturer and these engines are often fitted with much stronger connecting rods than the standard line of engine. If suitable heavy duty connecting rods are available, it makes good sense to fit them if the application warrants it. Bear in mind that occasional high rpm use is not the same as continuous high rpm use. Many road-going performance engines are operating nowhere near the maximum rpm they are capable of for 99% of the time and, occasional reasonably high rpm, seldom results in a broken connecting rod.

Racing and some other forms of motorsport are different as the engine is going to be turning between 5000 and 7000rpm most of the time and going to 8000 or 9000rpm, possibly more, at each gear change. Special connecting rods are normally required for this sort of treatment, but it's amazing how many racing engines actually do use standard connecting rods. Some factory made connecting rods are very strong. For example, the Sierra Cosworth connecting rod will withstand 9000rpm just as it comes. This is a bit of an exception perhaps, but there are mass production engines around that are very strong with excellent componentry inside them. The decision on whether to fit special heavy duty connecting rods should be based on the application and the known limitation of the particular standard connecting rods concerned.

The fitting of the lightest possible forged piston is a sure way to improve the reliability of any connecting rod, but within limits. These limits are the weight of the standard piston and piston pin versus the weight of the forged piston and piston pin. There can be savings of 100 to 200, or even 250, grams per piston and piston pin, making increases in engine rpm of between 300rpm to, perhaps, 500rpm relatively safe: it just depends on the connecting rods. Many modern standard engines have very light pistons fitted to them and weight savings are hard to make.

The forging flash of connecting rods can be ground and then polished off just to be sure that any forging imperfections that could lead to cracks forming are removed, but some connecting rods are so marginal in strength that no material should be removed. When material is removed from the I-beam of the connecting rod (0.005in/0.127mm, or so) the surface hardness formed during the forging process is also partially removed. If the connecting rod is quite substantial in the I-beam it can be cleaned up, polished and then shotpeened to restore surface hardness.

Shotpeening is a process whereby small metal balls are blasted against the surface of the (in this case) connecting rod. It has the effect of compressing the surface of the

connecting rod. Most connecting rods, in the interests of retaining the surface hardness caused by the forging process, and because of the minimal amount of material in the I-beam, are left just as they come, except for material removed for balancing purposes.

Heavy duty forged connecting rods are often very well finished with the forging flash having received extra treatment in the manufacturing process. These connecting rods, while being forged, have no real roughness along what is normally the roughly finished forging flash edge.

Many connecting rods are cast and, effectively, do not have a flash (they have a defined line along the I-beam of the connecting rod as they are formed in a mould). The trend is to leave the surface finish of these connecting rods just as it is. All connecting rods should be checked thoroughly. The checks involve a crack test, a straightness check (in both planes), small end diameter size check (for interference fit type piston pin retention rods), small end internal diameter and parallelism check and possible bush replacement for fully floating piston pins with circlip retention, big end diameter size check and a big end out of round check.

The connecting rods should be crack tested by an engine machine shop. The connecting rod is magnetized using an electro-magnet and while in this state a mixture of Magnaflux powder and paraffin (kerosene) is sprayed over it. If there is a crack, the powder will congregate along the crack and a 'black light' will highlight it. The operator must be skilled in the use of this equipment, as a crack can easily be missed. Any cracked component **must** be rejected and, ideally, scrapped so that it is out of the system forever. If one

connecting rod is cracked replace the whole set as, if one connecting rod is flawed through stress, the possibility exists that the other connecting rods may be close to a similar state: all components have a 'service life.'

Engines equipped with fully floating piston pins have connecting rods with bushed little (small) ends. These bushes are removable by pressing them out and new bushes can be pressed in which will restore the bush bore size. Bushes wear oval and become 'bell mouthed' - both problems being measurable with a telescopic gauge and an outside micrometer. The inside diameter of the little end bush is measured in the centre and at each end and in four positions radially. Connecting rods that need to have their little end bushing replaced should have the bushings

Inside diameter of a connecting rod's little end being measured with a telescopic gauge.

removed now, before any further checks are carried out. The new bushings are installed after the alignment test because if there is anything major wrong with the connecting rods (bent), they will be discarded.

After new bushes are pressed into the little end of the connecting rod and honed to size, the connecting rod alignment should be rechecked on a jig to make sure that it is still correct (there's room for error in the replacement bushing and honing process). Little end to piston pin running clearance varies manufacturer to manufacturer, but consider 0.0007in/0.018mm to be the minimum, 0.0015in/0.039mm to be the maximum and 0.001in/0.028mm to be optimum. The bore of the little end must be parallel.

To check alignment the connecting rod caps are now fitted (without the bearings) and then the rod placed on a connecting rod

Connecting rod alignment jig with a connecting rod having alignment checked in both planes at the same time.

alignment jig to check the alignment of the big and little ends in two planes. These machines are very accurate and can pick up misalignment down to 0.0001in/0.0025mm. An ideal set of connecting rods will be within 0.0005in/0.01mm in both planes. Many connecting rods will be found to be within 0.0005in/0.01mm, or less, in both planes. Straightening connecting rods is **not** recommended for high performance use. Replace any bent connecting rod with a good alternative.

The alignment jig does not check the length of the connecting rod. This is done off the machine with a vernier caliper. Vernier calipers are not all that accurate (within 0.001-0.002in/0.02-0.05mm), but are accurate enough to check rod length. The dimension, measured from the top of the big end bore to the bottom of the small end bore, should, effectively, be the same on all connecting rods.

If all of the connecting rods are identical in length, the set can generally be considered to be to specification.

True connecting rod length is actually measured from the centre of the big end to the centre of the small end. The true distance can be calculated by adding together half the diameter of the big end and half the diameter of the small end and then adding that dimension to the distance

Connecting rod being measured for length between the top of the big end tunnel and the bottom of the small end tunnel.

as measured from the top of the big end bore to the bottom of the small end bore. Engine machine shops usually have a catalogue which will list connecting rod centre to centre lengths.

The final test using the connecting rod alignment jig is carried out after the piston is fitted to the connecting rod. The jig allows alignment of the connecting rod and piston to be checked once assembled. This is necessary because, although the connecting rod has been thoroughly checked, the piston has not been checked. With the connecting rod known to be perfectly straight, if an error is found when the assembled piston and connecting rod is checked on the alignment jig, the error is caused by the piston.

PISTON PIN RETENTION AND LITTLE ENDS

There is some variation in how piston pins are retained in pistons, and this affects the connecting rod and is the reason why piston pin retention methods are described here. There are two basic methods of pin retention. The first is where the connecting rod little end can rotate in the bore of the connecting rod bush as well as within the piston's piston pin bore: this is termed 'fully floating' and means that the piston pin will be retained by circlips or Teflon buttons. The second method involves the interference fit of the piston pin in the bore of the little end of the connecting rod. The little end of the connecting rod is very slightly smaller in diameter than the piston pin (which therefore has to be press fitted) or the little end is split on one side and has a clamp bolt (eg. BMC A-series engines). The piston pin can only oscillate in the piston pin bore. This system is reliable, long lasting and makes for a rigid assembly.

Circlip piston pin retention

Older engines featured stamped circlips which fitted into square-cornered grooves in the piston pin bore of the piston at each end of the piston pin. A variation of this system (in the interests of reliability) uses two circlips of the same type and size each side of the piston pin, but in a wider square-cornered groove. Pressed circlips should be fitted with the sharp edge (formed by the metal pressing process) facing the bore wall, meaning that the sharp edge fits right into the corner of the groove in the piston, so giving maximum circlip to piston contact.

While pressed steel circlip piston pin retention is suitable for moderate high performance applications, it is less than ideal and cannot be regarded as being fail safe. The usual scenario with this type of circlip pin retention is that the groove wears widthwise as the ends of the piston pin 'move' back and forth against the circlips, this is compounded by the fact that this type of circlip does not exert a lot of radial tension and therefore tends to be rotated in its groove. The overall effect is that the groove does not remain as originally machined and, once there is any appreciable sideways and radial circlip movement, reliability of the retention system is questionable.

Other engine designs feature a single round wire circlip in a half round

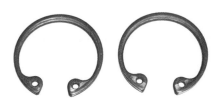

Stamped steel circlips.

groove in the piston pin bore. These wire circlips sometimes have a tang on one end to facilitate installation and removal. These tangs have been known to break off (usually caused by being reused). The tang is slightly angled in relation to the main body of the circlip and **must** lean outward towards the bore wall. To check which way the tangs are angled, place all of the circlips on a flat surface. If the tang is facing down the circlip will not sit flat and will rock.

Caution! - circlips of any description can only be used once and if the groove in the piston pin bore is damaged in any way, the circlip can come out of the groove in use.

Stamped steel circlips or wire circlips with tangs are not really suitable for high-performance use (even though the stamped steel circlip *is* frequently used) because, overall, they are not really reliable long term. It is usual for the machined groove in the aluminium of the piston to become burred and wider than when first machined: this leads to the problem of piston pin removal.

To facilitate removal of a piston pin from a burred piston pin bore once the circlips have been removed, insert a square-ended piston pin-sized mandrel (turned up in a lathe) or another piston pin into the piston pin bore and swage the displaced aluminium back into the groove. The piston pin can then be removed reasonably easily but will need to be lightly tapped out (use plenty of oil).

There is a derivative of the wire circlip that is now used and favoured for competition and is regarded as being 'bullet proof'. This is a very strong round wire circlip which has no tang; instead there's a slot in the piston to facilitate removal of the circlip. The ends of the piston pin are either square and have point contact

Round wire circlips with no tang. Wire diameters usually range from 0.060in/ 1.5mm to 0.070in/1.8mm.

with the circlip at the piston pin diameter, or feature chamfers 0.040in/ 1.0mm wide at 45 degrees and have point contact with the circlip at a diameter smaller than the piston pin diameter, a feature which tends to push the circlip into its groove. There are pros and cons with either design. The square-ended piston pin type see the piston pin fitted into the piston with the absolute minimum of endfloat (about 0.003in/0.075mm). The chamfered end piston pin type has to have considerably more endfloat by way of the fact that to fit the circlips with the piston pin installed the reduction in effective overall length of the piston pin caused by the chamfer is not taken into account. The endfloat using this system is approximately 0.040in/1.0mm. Most forged racing pistons use round wire circlip retention and are reliable.

The advantage of circlip type retention methods is the ease (well, comparative ease, anyway) with which the piston and connecting rod assembly can be dismantled and assembled. Seldom, though, can the piston pin be removed without some force as almost always there will be a burr thrown up on the outer edge of the circlip groove. Round grooves - as opposed to square - while still being prone to losing their size through sideways impact from the piston pin, maintain their groove size longer than other designs.

Small end bore of a connecting rod being measured with a telescopic gauge. Once the size is taken, an outside micrometer is used to measure across the telescopic gauge to 0.0001in/0.0025mm accuracy.

When the circlip grooves are no longer on size, the pistons can't be used with circlip retention of the piston pin but an alternative is to use Teflon buttons. Teflon buttons (which are custom machined out of bar stock) locate in the piston pin bore at each end of the piston pin. The disadvantage of Teflon buttons is that they do wear away, which means that there is a time limit before there is no piston pin retention! The rate of wear varies from engine to engine, so hard and fast rules cannot be applied. Suffice it to say that, if the pistons are slab sided (unusual in a four cylinder engine) the rate of wear can be monitored by removing the sump (oil pan) and inspecting the amount of Teflon button remaining by looking through the crankcase. By noting the distance covered and the rate of wear from new, a clear indication of the rate of button wear on the particular engine can be accurately judged. If the buttons have 0.008in/0.20mm endfloat when new the amount of wear can be quite easily measured with a feeler gauge. Teflon buttons will shine the sides of the bore where they rub, but they will not normally wear

the bore measurably. Because Teflon buttons can wear out in as little as 1000miles/1600km the reality is that, for most engines, Teflon buttons are only suitable for competition use (the engine will be frequently stripped and mileages are not high).

Caution! - Never re-use Teflon buttons. Dirt particles get into engine oil one way or another and, if these particles embed themselves into the relatively soft Teflon, the ends of the buttons will tend to score (in a minor way) the cylinder bore. This bore 'shininess' can affect ring seal and ring seating as it can't be honed out but this is a minor problem in the overall scheme of things.

Interference fit piston pin retention

The method which is now widely favoured for production car engines is press fit, or interference fit, of the piston pin into the bore of the connecting rod. The only disadvantage of this system is that when the pistons have to be removed from the connecting rods, a press is required, and the piston may well end up irreparably damaged. However, this is not really a serious problem as the pistons are usually removed for replacement. There's no doubt that for long term permanent piston pin retention this method is ideal (no circlips to come out, which will allow the piston pin to move and contact the bore wall). There is also minimal piston movement except for the required swing action of the connecting rod. There are no real downsides to using this type of piston pin retention system and it is very reliable. This system normally only fails when the interference fit sizing between the piston pin and the small end of the connecting rod is

insufficient (less than 0.0002in/ 0.006mm.)

A press fit (interference fit) between the piston pin and the small end means that the piston pin has to be 0.0005-0.0008in/0.013-0.02mm larger than the small end diameter in the connecting rod. The maximum amount of difference allowable between the piston pin and the small end of a connecting rod is 0.0015in/ 0.042mm. The majority of small end bores to piston pin fits will be 0.0005in/0.013mm.

The sizes of connecting rod small end bores varies within the range 0.0005-0.001in/0.0127-0.025mm which is a tolerance of 0.0005in/ 0.0123mm. The size of piston pins varies (by as much as 0.0003in/ 0.0076mm) too and so it's possible to have a piston pin and connecting rod small end combination that has virtually no interference fit. Check all piston pin sizes and all connecting rod small end diameters to ensure that an adequate interference fit is present.

Match the piston pin sizes of the piston set to a connecting rod small end bore diameter that gives the maximum interference fit for each combination. By selectively matching the piston pins to the connecting rod small ends, the optimum available interference fit will be present in each connecting rod and piston pin combination.

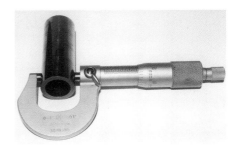

Piston pin being accurately measured with an outside micrometer. Measurements need to be within 0.0001in/0.0025mm.

Measure the connecting rod's small end diameters before the piston set is purchased. This way, the minimum acceptable size of wrist pin will be known before the piston set is paid for and taken away. Wrist pin sizes do vary by as much as 0.0002in/0.005mm so the amount of variation possible in interference fit can be quite significant.

If the inside diameter of the small end is no longer on size, the connecting rod will have to be replaced if the interference retention method is used.

Note that the internal surface of the connecting rod's small end **must** have a honed finish.

Caution! - Do **not** use any connecting rod that has visible signs of overheating (connecting rods are often heated to facilitate fitting and removal of pistons) as the material could be 'soft' and will not hold the interference fit. Pistons and connecting rods that use interference fit piston pin retention should have pistons removed and fitted using a connecting rod heater (an induction heater used to heat the little end of the connecting rod in a controlled manner with no possibility of overheating), or using a press with suitable jigging to prevent galling.

CONNECTING ROD BIG END TUNNEL RESIZING

High-performance engines must have the big end bores (or tunnels) of the connecting rods resized to ensure that the big end bore diameter is perfectly round and, equally important, that the size of the big end bore diameter is on 'nominal size' or, better still, 'bottom size.' This is to ensure that the two big end bearing shells are held in the big end bore with the maximum bearing crush possible within the factory tolerance.

Interference fit type connecting rod bolt being removed using a concave faced punch. Connecting rod is firmly held in a vice (with protective jaws fitted to prevent surface damage to the sides of the connecting rod).

Not all connecting rods can have the big end bore resized. The serrated part-line type of connecting rod, for instance, cannot easily be remachined on the part-line and, as a consequence, such connecting rods are simply replaced when the big end bore is out of tolerance.

The factory specifications will list a 'nominal size' for the big end. The factory sizes also have a plus and a minus tolerance on the 'nominal size.' The plus tolerance size is called 'top size' and the minus size is called 'bottom size.'

A big end bore on 'top size' would see the bearing crush as measured with a feeler gauge down to zero or 0.001in/0.0025mm and this is an insufficient amount of crush for high performance use. **Caution!** -

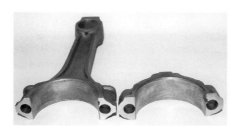

Cap and the connecting rod matching surfaces that have had material removed from them. The connecting rod bolts have to be removed from the connecting rod to accomplish this.

Under no circumstances should a connecting rod be used with such a small amount of crush. Consider the minimum amount of crush to be 0.003in/0.075mm.

When connecting rods which have fitted bolts are resized, the fitted bolts are removed from the connecting rod and both the cap and connecting rod matching faces are reground (not just the cap because it is easier!) Removing the bolts can be quite difficult but suffice to say all bolts can be removed one way or another. The bolts that are being replaced are removed now, before the big end is resized.

During resizing a minimal amount of material is ground from the cap, connecting rod and bore but always sufficient to clean the surface up 100%. Depending on how much error there is to be corrected in the big end bore, the amount removed from each is usually between 0.001-0.002in/0.025mm-0.050mm.

Note that a connecting rod big end bore *can* be restored by removing material from the cap's matching surface alone and not removing the connecting rod bolts but, unless the matching surface of the connecting rod is machined, the integrity (flatness) of that surface remains an unknown factor and, for this reason, this method is **not** recommended.

After the matching surfaces have been reground (on any connecting rod) the edges of the connecting rod and cap are hand-filed to clean them up. Use fine needle files to do this. The edges should have a 0.005in/0.125mm chamfer on them when finished. This chamfer represents the removal of the sharp edge only. Any burring of edges or slivers of steel can prevent the surfaces from matching properly and bearing crush will be reduced, which could result in a

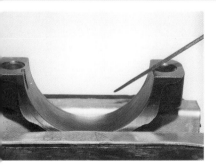

Edges of the connecting rod cap faces being filed with a needle file.

Edges of a connecting rod being filed with a needle file.

ap part line faces that have been neatly chamfered with a needle file.

aring failure. Detailing like this is not solutely necessary, but it is desirable d recommended. If the connecting d does not need to be resized the atching surface edges should still be nd-filed to clean them up and to move sharp edges.

When installing interference fit olts into connecting rods, the new olts are fitted using an aluminium or

copper drift punch. For ease of fitting the connecting rod can be placed onto a piece of 1in by 1in or 25mm by 25mm aluminium which has had two clearance holes for the connecting rod bolts drilled in it. The connecting rod sits on top of the aluminium square bar and the bolts move through the drilled holes as they are driven into the connecting rod. Aluminium is used for the assembly jig as it will not mark the very important matching surface of the connecting rod.

Make sure that the head of each bolt is positioned correctly so that

Aluminium block assembly jig used to assist with the installation of interference fit type connecting rod bolts. Note that the aluminium has had one side machined so that a ridge is formed which prevents the aluminium block from moving downwards in the vice.

when it is fully home there is no doubt that the whole head of the bolt is in contact with the surface of the connecting rod machined recess. **Caution!** - There is quite a range of bolt head styles but, irrespective of the head style, the head of the bolt **must**

Head of the connecting rod bolt in square on contact with the connecting rod's machined recess.

Connecting rod being held in a vice with protective shields over the jaws to protect the sides of the connecting rod from being damaged. The rod is held as close to the partline as possible: this is the only acceptable way to hold the connecting rod when the nuts are being torqued.

be in full contact with the connecting rod spot facing (broached surface).

Fit the cap to the connecting rod and torque the retaining nuts (or bolts) to the correct tension. It is acceptable to tap the cap home, but ensure the matching faces stay parallel at all times.

Six point socket in full contact with the nut; the outside diameter of the socket is just clear of the cap's machined recess. It would not take a much larger diameter socket to cause interference with the cap and the result can be a misaligned cap.

Note that some sockets are not slimline and will not clear the cap sufficiently, causing slight misalignment. Make sure that the socket fits over the nut and does not interfere with the cap.

Connecting rods that have the cap located by small dowels are quite common. Connecting rods using this form of cap location use bolts (screws) only to retain the cap. The bolts can be replaced at any time without the danger of cap misalignment because they do not locate the cap. When the big end bore is resized, the two locating dowels must be removed so that the matching surfaces can be reground. Small hollow dowels are often difficult to remove: the usual method is to insert the tang of a small

Small hollow dowel method of cap location with bolt (screw) retention.

drill which is 0.002in-0.003in/0.050-0.075mm smaller than the inside bore size of the dowel, and then squeeze the dowel in a vice which has non-serrated jaws. This is to prevent the dowel from being damaged and yet squeezed sufficiently (effectively made smaller) to facilitate its removal. The connecting rod or cap can then be oscillated back and forth by hand and once seen to be moving, axial force, as well as the oscillating motion, is used to pull the cap or connecting rod away from the dowel. **Caution!** - The same dowels usually have to be refitted after the matching surfaces have been remachined as it is virtually impossible to buy replacement dowels from parts

Small hollow dowel being removed from a connecting rod.

suppliers - so take care when removing dowels. If a dowel does get damaged, a good source for a replacement is another connecting rod of the same type.

Some late model production engines use precision ground bolts (without nuts), which are not an interference fit, to retain and locate the connecting rod cap. The holes in the cap are precision machined. The whole deal relies on all of the parts involved being dead accurate in size. The bolts must be the correct diameter size and parallel, the holes in the cap must be the correct diameter size and parallel, the holes and the threads in

the connecting rod must not be damaged in any way. The manufacture of connecting rods using this type of cap location is a precision exercise, to say the least. When assembled the big end bore of rods using this system is checked the same as any other connecting rod.

Big end bore honing
The big end bore is honed to size on machine which is designed specifical for this operation. This process will se the big end bore resized to 'nominal' or 'bottom' size and the aperture will be perfectly round without any distortion (ovality, humps or hollows

If it is decided not to resize the connecting rod big ends, the cap and connecting rod matching surfaces should be cleaned up on a true flat surface (surface plate) which has a sheet of 180 grit wet and dry paper placed on it. This does not apply to interference fit bolt-type connecting rods as to remove and replace the bolts can mean that the cap no longe lines up properly (which would be cured by resizing) but, at the very least, the cap alone can be cleaned u

The cap and connecting rod are in turn moved back and forth (not radially) over the abrasive paper unti

A connecting rod's big end bore being honed. The connecting rod is removed from the machine periodically to be accurately measured with an inside micrometer.

An inside micrometer being used to check the diameter of the big end bore in the vertical plane.

The big end bore being measured at 60 degrees to the right of the vertical plane.

The big end bore being measured at 60 degrees to the left of the vertical plane.

leaned up. Firm hand pressure is required to hold the surfaces down square on to the flat surface. A

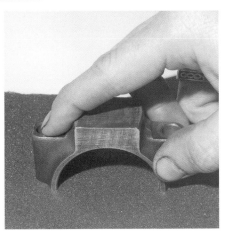

A cap being cleaned up by the abrasive action of rubbing it back and forth over a sheet of wet and dry paper placed on the top of a surface plate (or plate glass).

A connecting rod being cleaned up on a surface plate. Great care must be taken to ensure that the connecting rod is held firmly and squarely against the flat surface.

minimal amount of material will be removed but sufficient to clean the surface up 100%. This process will ensure that the two matching surfaces are in full contact with each other when the cap is bolted on to the connecting rod. The edges of the cap and connecting rod matching faces should be chamfered 0.005in/0.13mm and new bolts fitted to the connecting rod, the cap fitted and the bolts torqued in the normal manner (clamped in a vice). Measure the inside diameter of the big end bore in three different positions.

If the measurements are different it's an indication of ovality or cap misalignment, or both. If there is inaccuracy there is **no** alternative but to resize the big end.

Although this method of cleaning up the matching faces combined with new bolts is very often completely satisfactory, the recommendation is still to resize the big end.

CONNECTING ROD BOLTS

Stock connecting rod bolts are **always** replaced.

The usual range of connecting rod bolt sizes is 5/16in/8mm, 11/32in/9mm, 3/8in/9.55mm in diameter.

Any engine that is being built up with a performance orientation should have high strength aftermarket connecting rod bolts fitted. These bolts are definitely stronger and rated at around 190,000 pounds per square

A range of connecting rod bolts, left to right: a 3/8in bolt, a 5/16in nut and bolt, an 8mm bolt, a 9mm nut and bolt.

inch tensile strength.

When new interference fit-type bolts are fitted the big end bore will usually need to be resized (depends on the design of the connecting rod). The reason for this is that when the new bolts are installed, the cap may not fit in exactly the same position as it previously did. This problem does not apply to serrated part-line, doweled or the more modern bolt-located connecting rod caps.

Obviously, the position of the cap will be very close to original and the amount of error will be very small (0.001in-0.002in/0.02mm-0.04mm at the most), but it only takes one big end bore to be out and unchecked to lead to engine failure!

If a cap does not line up, the bearings will not be held in a perfect circle or may be slightly staggered. Either way, the situation is not correct and will have to be rectified. All connecting rod big end bores should be remachined (honed) to remove all possibility of cap misalignment and tunnel bore distortion, and to ensure optimum inside diameter so that the shells are held in a perfectly round and parallel bore with the correct amount of crush.

Note that connecting rod bolts must be changed frequently in competition engines to avoid breakage. The fitting of new bolts or bolts and nuts is regarded as good insurance against breakage, but not an absolute guarantee.

Checking connecting rod bolts for stretch

Torquing nuts a prescribed tightness is just a convenient way of setting the bolt with the amount of tension that stretches the bolt within its elastic limits. This means that if the tension is removed from the bolt (nut removed or the bolt undone), the bolt will

New connecting rod bolt being measured for length.

Bolt torqued to prescribed seting and then measured again.

return to its original size provided the elastic limit of the material is not exceeded. Most bolt threads must be lubed before the nut is put on.

When tightening connecting rod nuts always check to see that the socket does not interfere with the side of the connecting rod cap: check on each connecting rod. Once satisfied that there is no contact, keep the socket specifically for this operation so that there is no chance of another, similar, socket (which may not clear the cap) being used.

Measure all bolt lengths as they come out of the packet and compare those individual measurements against the new lengths when the bolts are subject to correct torque. All bolts must take the prescribed torque and not stretch more than the specified amount. Expect the bolt to stretch between 0.006in-0.008in/0.15mm-0.20mm (depends on the bolt).

The amount of stretch for the particular aftermarket bolt will be listed in the fitting instructions that come with the bolts. If a bolt takes the prescribed torque but stretches well

beyond the listed limit, that bolt should not be used in an engine.

On odd occasions a new bolt will not take the prescribed torque setting. For instance if the torque requirement is 35Ib.ft/103Nm, yet the bolt won't go over, say, 18-22Ib.ft/80-86Nm, check the length of the bolt against its original size. Expect the bolt to be about 0.030in/0.75mm longer before you notice that it is not taking the torque. The most likely reason for the bolt failure is incorrect heat treatment. Replace the bolt. Any bolt (or nut and bolt) can be checked in this manner unless the bolt screws into a blind hole. If a bolt or nut and bolt will not take the prescribed torque it is faulty and **must** be discarded. **Caution!** - Do not continue with the engine assembly until satisfactory bolts are available.

AFTERMARKET CONNECTING RODS

The manufacturers of these connecting rods (which are almost all forged) guarantee the accuracy of the product as the factory quality control system is virtually fail-safe. Even so, it is recommended that all such rods be checked for straightness, little end bore diameter and big end bore diameter. While expensive, high strength rods are exceedingly durable and virtually unbreakable but they are seldom really necessary for anything other than a racing engine. All engine components have a fatigue life, and even the very best aftermarket connecting rods have a limit! They are not an absolute guarantee against rod failure.

Used aftermarket heavy-duty connecting rods should be checked and rebuilt if necessary in just the same way as used stock type connecting rods. This will include

Heavy duty standard original equipment connecting rod.

principles of 'check fitting' remain the same for any connecting rod.

BEARING CRUSH

With rod tunnels resized to 'nominal size' or 'bottom size' and new connecting rod bolts fitted, the new replacement bearing shells can be 'check fitted' into the connecting rods and the amount of bearing crush determined.

Thoroughly clean the backs of the bearing shells and the tunnel surfaces of the connecting rods using a solvent. Install the shells in the cap and connecting rod, fit the cap to the rod and torque the nuts up. Hold the connecting rod in a vice equipped with soft jaws (to protect the side faces of the connecting rod) and make sure the connecting rod is held as close to the part line as possible.

The next step is to undo one nut (or bolt) to remove tension from that side of the connecting rod. The shells exert a radial force which causes this side of the cap to lift. The gap is measurable with a feeler gauge and is termed the 'crush height.' Expect the gap to be anything from 0.004-0.006in/0.10-0.15mm. If the tunnel is on 'bottom size' and there is 0.001in/0.03mm crush height, the shells are faulty (rare, but possible).

If some connecting rod bearing shell combinations give varying 'crush heights,' such as some having 0.006in/0.15mm and others 0.003in/0.75mm, mix and match the shell halves to see if the crush heights can be evened up. There is frequently some slight variation between the shells. This means, for example, swapping a shell half from a 0.006in/0.15mm crush height connecting rod into a 0.003in/0.75mm crush height connecting rod combination which will alter the crush height of both connecting rods,

Connecting rod held in soft vice jaws and both nuts torqued to prescribed setting.

With the new bearing shells fitted and after torquing both nuts, one nut is then undone.

especially if the connecting rod tunnel sizes are all identical.

If it proves impossible to establish sufficient crush height at this stage, the shells are almost certainly faulty and should be replaced by another set. It is also wise to double-check the tunnel sizes.

OPTIMUM BIG END BEARING CLEARANCE

Smaller four cylinder engines have big end journals of around 1.625in/41.2mm diameter and require big end bearing clearances of 0.0017in-0.0019in/0.046mm-0.050mm, while larger four cylinder engines have big end journals of around 2.000in/51.0mm diameter and require a bearing clearance of 0.0023-0.0025in/0.057-0.062mm.

crack testing, straightness testing, big end resizing, little end bore diameter and parallelism check (possible bush replacement) and fitting new connecting rod bolts.

All aftermarket connecting rods (new or used) have to have the bearings check fitted into them to ensure that bearing crush is correct and that the inside diameter of the bearing bore is compatible with the crankshaft journal diameter. All other aspects of 'check fitting' these connecting rods into an engine block are the same as for the stock type of connecting rod. The wrist pin retention method may vary by way of being a press fit or fully floating, but the basic

Bearing tunnel of connecting rod being measured with an inside micrometer. The first measurement is taken vertically.

Inside micrometer measuring the bearing bore 60 degrees to the right of vertical.

Inside micrometer measuring the bearing bore 60 degrees to the left of vertical.

BIG END BEARING DIAMETERS

With the crush heights checked and all connecting rods having similar measurements, the nuts are torqued again and the bearing bore diameters accurately measured with an inside micrometer. Usually all of the connecting rod big end bearing bores will be 'in tolerance,' which means all bores being within 0.0002in/0.006mm of each other.

The inside diameter of a bearing is measured in three places to check that the bearing is round overall and on size.

The sizes measured are recorded and checked against the factory specification. The desired bearing clearance is then deducted from the bearing's internal diameter to give the correct crankshaft journal size.

If the desired clearance is not obtainable the problem lies with the crankshaft journal size or the size of the bearing bore. Double-check all sizes to find out which components are not to size. Because of manufacturing tolerances both may be wrong and generally the crankshaft journal will be 'eased' (ground down) to suit the bearing bore size to fix the problem. All sizes **must** be within tolerance.

If the crankshaft is to be reground, now that the connecting rods are refurbished and the actual connecting rod bearing sizes are known, the crankshaft journals can be ground to suit - individually, if necessary. If the connecting rod bearing bores were resized so that the bearing has the maximum amount of crush, the size of the bearing bore will usually be on or near minimum size. The crankshaft may also have to be ground to the minimum size or 'bottom size' within the factory tolerances.

Chapter 8
Crankshaft

The ideal used crankshaft is one that is crack free, standard in journal size and needing only a journal polish. It is not uncommon to find crankshafts in this condition, despite the fact that many older engines or well used ones receive virtually no oil and filter changes and are very dirty inside.

If a crankshaft has been damaged through a bearing failure it will almost always need to be reground. When contemplating regrinding a crankshaft, the diameter of the connecting rod journals is more critical than the main bearing diameter, simply because the mains are always larger in diameter and, as a consequence, stronger. It is acceptable to regrind main bearings to 0.060in/1.50mm undersize, but consider 0.020in/0.50mm the **maximum** undersize when regrinding connecting rod journals for anything other than a stock engine. A racing engine should have a new crankshaft with standard sized journals but 0.010in/0.025mm undersize on both

main and big end journals is acceptable but, generally, certainly not more, especially the big ends. The surface finish of the journals is vital: they **must** be smooth and polished.

The connecting rod bearing bores have already been measured, so the ideal sizes to achieve the desired bearing running clearance for the crankshaft big end journals is known.

CHECKING THE CRANKSHAFT

The external surfaces of the crankshaft must be 100% crack tested with special attention being paid to each journal's fillet radius (corner radius). Crankshafts crack in many places but by far the most common is in the corner radius of a journal, especially the rearmost big end journal. Any crankshaft that has a crack **must** be replaced. Crack testing equipment, as used by engine reconditioners, can only check the surface of the

crankshaft for cracks.

The crankshaft is magnetized by an electro-magnet and a mixture of 'Magnaflux' powder and paraffin (kerosene) is sprayed over it. If there is a crack the powder will congregate along the crack and highlight it. The operator must be skilled in the use of this equipment as a crack can easily be missed. The crankshaft is demagnetized after the crack test procedure.

The fact that a crankshaft passes the crack test does not mean that it is totally crack-free: this type of equipment will not pick up an internal crack. The only way to check a crankshaft 100% is to have it X-rayed. Cracks can start inside the crankshaft from the drilled oil holes. A crack testing procedure can only show that, at the time of the test, the crankshaft was crack-free. A crankshaft can develop cracks shortly after it is put back in service. Having a crankshaft pass a crack test is not a guarantee

Centre main bearing being checked for runout. The front and rear bearings only are installed. Main caps are all fully torqued as per normal.

Die grinder with a 3/16in diameter mounted point being used to smooth off a sharp edge. Be quite generous with the radius if the journal is going to be reground as the radius will get smaller as the grinding proceeds.

Pair of old shells have been taped onto the journal surface so that the surfaces are protected while the crankshaft is rotary wire brushed.

that it will not crack and break in service.

The crankshaft must be straightness tested between centres of a lathe or in a crankshaft grinder. This check can also be carried out using the engine block with the front and rear bearing shells only fitted: a dial indicator and magnetic stand can be used to check the runout of each main journal. **Caution!** - Engines with centre thrusts must have buffer material in place of the thrust bearing to prevent possible damage to the crankshaft thrust surfaces when the crankshaft is turned.

CRANKSHAFT PREPARATION

If the crankshaft does not need to be reground, measure the crankshaft journals with a micrometer to check that they are on size and perfectly round. Measure each of the journals in

six different places to be certain that there is no ovality.

The oilways **must** be radiused where they exit at the journal surfaces (main and big end bearings). Frequently the edge formed by the hole as it breaks out on to the journal surface is razor sharp - particularly after a regrind.

A high speed die grinder with a 3/16in/4mm diameter mounted point is the ideal tool to do this job. Work slowly with minimal side pressure on the stone to avoid slipping and running over the journal surface. Care is needed when grinding to avoid slipping and damaging the bearing surface even if the crankshaft is going to be reground.

Crankshaft's unmachined surfaces being rotary wire brushed. Take precautions against contacting the journal surfaces as they can be marked and this will be a problem if the journals are not going to be reground.

If the journal is on size and does not need to be reground, the oil holes will have to be ground very carefully to avoid the high speed grinder slipping and marking the journal surface. **Caution!** - One slip with the grinder and the journal surface will be marked: absolute care is vital.

Clean all unmachined surfaces (all cast or forged surfaces) with a rotary wire brush to remove all dirt and grime. If the crankshaft has been cleaned in a hot tank, there will be very little to clean off.

The journal surfaces should be completely masked by placing a pair of old bearing shells onto the journal surface and then wrapping electrical tape around the outside of the shells to hold the shells in place. If you slip with the rotary wire brush it will run across the tape and the back of a bearing shell.

Crankshaft journal being measured with a micrometer.

Casting flash being removed, or smoothed, on a typical crankshaft.

Tap and tap wrench being used to clean out a thread hole in the rear flange of a crankshaft.

Journal which has been radius rolled in manufacture.

Scour all oilways with a square-ended mild steel rod to remove all traces of dirt and grime. An engine that has not had regular oil changes will most likely have considerable build-up in the oilways. The mild steel rod will not damage the inside of the crankshaft oilways.

Remove all casting or forging flash. Most crankshafts have rough edges on them which can be quite sharp and, more to the point, loose. The crankshaft surfaces can be detailed using a high speed grinder and a mounted point stone. All edges that have been ground should be further smoothed over by hand using 320 grit wet and dry paper or cloth tape.

Smooth off all surface irregularities at the casting part lines and around holes in the throws of the crankshaft.

Clean out the threaded holes in the rear crankshaft flange with a tap.

Threaded holes that go right through the flange have to be sealed against oil leaks; the tap clears out the old sealer and retaps the holes so that the crankshaft or flywheel bolts can be wound in easily and torqued without interference from distorted threads.

There is no substitute for a crankshaft that is dead straight, has perfectly round journals, precise clearances on each and every bearing combination, well radiused oilways and flawless surface finish on each of the journal surfaces. The as-cast or forged surfaces of the crankshaft have been smoothed over using the high speed grinder and mounted point grinding stone. It should be impossible to cut yourself on the crankshaft after it has been detailed.

CRANKSHAFT REGRINDING

Engine machine shops use a specification book that lists all crankshaft sizes and the permissible tolerances on those sizes. This means that the machine shop can regrind a crankshaft to book sizes and know that the clearances will be quite satisfactory for normal purposes. This is all very well for a stock engine but, for a high performance engine, it's desirable to take more trouble in the interests of reliability and reduced frictional losses.

Optimum crankshaft journal sizes are ascertained by measuring the bearing shell bores as described previously and subtracting the desired running clearance: the result is the required journal size (individual, if necessary).

Before regrinding the crankshaft, the oilway exits should be radiused where they meet the journal surface.

When regrinding a crankshaft the big end journals are always ground first (if they are being reground). The reason for this is that there can be slight flexing of the crankshaft during regrinding and, if this happens, when the mains have already been finished the crankshaft will not run true: in extreme cases the mains may have to be reground to a further undersize to correct the situation. Crankshaft journal surfaces need to have as near a mirror finish as possible.

Not all engine machine shops put a nice fillet radius on the corners of each journal, so each corner should be checked to see how good the radius is before the crankshaft is taken away from the workshop. Discuss this feature with the engine machine shop personnel before work commences, and insist that each corner radius be a full radius which blends smoothly from the journal surface in to the sides of the crankshaft throws. **Caution!** - If a step or edge is formed during the

Positions of the feeler gauges when the cap bolts are being torqued.

regrinding process this will act as a stress point which could lead to crankshaft failure.

Many late model engine crankshafts have journals with rolled radii. This is ideal and it takes about 0.040in/0.10mm undersize grinding of the journal before the radii are lost. Crankshafts like this are strongest with the rolled radius in place.

Check fitting the connecting rods to the crankshaft

With the crankshaft reground, or if the journals did not require regrinding and were polished only, the connecting rods are check fitted to the crankshaft to make sure that the desired clearances are present.

In the first instance, each connecting rod is fitted to its respective journal. If there is anything wrong, such as insufficient bearing clearance (connecting rod cannot be rotated 360 degrees easily) or connecting rod side clearance it will be found now and can be corrected at this point.

With the crankshaft lying on a bench, each connecting rod is fitted to its journal and torqued up just as it would be when assembled in the block. Do not apply engine oil to the journals and the bearing surfaces at this point. **Caution!** - Before the connecting rod bolts are torqued up, insert a feeler gauge between the connecting rod and the crankshaft

journal face to prevent any sideways twisting movement of the connecting rods; use the same method when the nuts are undone.

Note that by placing a correctly sized feeler gauge between the connecting rod and crankshaft face the side clearance is also ascertained. The side clearance must be within the stock tolerance limits, not too tight and not too loose. Seldom will the connecting rod side clearances be less than 0.008in/0.20mm or more than 0.010in/0.25mm. Check all side clearances to the manufacturer's specifications. The side clearances do **not** need to be greater than the maximum factory size. In fact, it's desirable that the clearances are not more than the maximum factory recommended size. Replace the offending part/s if the clearance is too great.

Caution! - Do not rotate the connecting rods on the crankshaft journals until the nuts are torqued. The reason for this is that, until the nuts are torqued up, the two shells have not been forced to take the shape of the connecting rod tunnel and the surfaces of the bearing shells can be damaged by rotation.

Caution! - Check that the socket used to tighten the nuts does not contact the connecting rod cap: if it does, the cap can become misaligned.

With the connecting rods fitted, the crankshaft is lifted up so that it is vertical (rested on the rear flange), or its snout is clamped in a vice with protective shields fitted between the vice jaws and the snout.

The connecting rods are then individually checked for freedom of rotation for the full 360 degrees available. By turning the connecting rods one at a time any binding will be felt.

If there is binding, remove that

Crankshaft lying on a bench top with a connecting rod fitted to the front journal

particular connecting rod, refit the cap and then remeasure the bearing shell bore diameter in three places and especially where there are scuff marks. This is to check the overall roundness of the bearing bore. Check also for misalignment of the cap caused by the socket becoming jammed against the connecting rod cap.

If there is binding there will be some scuffing of the bearing shell surface but it can be very difficult to see at times: use a magnifying glass if necessary.

Bearing shells can have high spots but it is unusual. If there is a high spot it can be eased with a three-cornered scraper, but **never** with abrasive paper. Before scraping check to make sure that it really is a high spot and not a lack of bearing clearance.

With this procedure carried out and the bearing clearances proved correct, or found to be incorrect and the situation remedied, the connecting rod to crankshaft check fitting is complete.

Tight bearing clearances are not desirable. If the bearing bore diameters are known before the crankshaft is reground there are definite sizes to which to grind the crankshaft. This is the correct way of obtaining the correct running bearing clearance and it is a logical sequence requiring the least work.

FLYWHEEL DOWELLING

If the flywheel is going to be dowelled this is the time to do it. Engines have varying numbers of flywheel retention bolts, ranging from one large bolt to four, six and nine bolts. The more bolts the better for high performance use. Some engines with flywheels which have only four or six bolt retention sometimes have the bolts come loose, but this only happens with modified engines. The generally accepted solution to this problem is to dowel the flywheel to the crankshaft and so remove the radial location of

the flywheel from the bolts. This means that the dowel or dowels take the shock loadings and the bolts are used only to retain the flywheel.

There is some complication in dowelling the crankshaft and flywheel in terms of getting everything lined up. The usual machinery used to do this work sees the crankshaft mounted on a radial drill or a horizontal boring machine. These are large machines found only in engineering works that do heavy engineering or large precision work.

Flywheels are usually drilled and reamed to accept one, two or three dowels, but any number of dowels that can be accommodated in the crankshaft/flywheel without unduly weakening it are okay. One good sized dowel (3/8in/10mm) is often enough but frequently dowels are 5/16in/8mm in diameter, in which case the usual number of dowels used is three. The most common procedure sees the flywheel marked with a pitch circle

(usually the same as the bolt pitch circle) and the number of dowels to be fitted have their positions marked with a centre dot on the pitch circle. With the work firmly clamped on the machine the holes are then drilled (undersize) and reamed to size. The holes are reamed tight (well used reamer) to suit the dowels so that they are very tight when fitted to the flywheel. The fit of the dowels in the flywheel does not have to be quite so tight as the flywheel has to come off relatively easily. The reamed holes in the flywheel are eased using an 'on size' reamer.

Dowels are made from high tensile steel and are case hardened. All engineering workshops use dowels and they are readily available in varying lengths (imperial and metric sizes) the shortest being 0.75in/20mm through to 1.5in/35mm. They can be cut (parted off) or ground down.

Chapter 9
Engine balance

The rebalancing of the engine components is specialist work. The principles and the sequence only are described here.

Engines are generally very well balanced as they come from their respective manufacturers. There will always be the possibility of getting an engine that is not well balanced through a bad combination of production tolerances and variances, but this is exceedingly unlikely because the design and relative weights of the components preclude this happening. Some engines will be better balanced than others. Most engines will be found to be within the factory specifications and, as a consequence, balanced within very tight limits and most certainly suitable for operation up to 7000rpm. It is very unusual to find an engine produced these days that is grossly out of balance as it comes from the factory.

When a four cylinder engine is designed the weight of the pistons, rings, piston pins and connecting rods is all taken into account and the crankshaft will have partial counter-weighting or full counter-weighting (full counter-weighting being the current trend).

If an engine is to be perfectly balanced, each piston, rings and piston pin set must be within one gram of the others. The connecting rods must be balanced end for end and weight for weight to within one gram of each other. The crankshaft is then 'run up' on a dynamic balancing machine and the amount of imbalance (if any) measured and material is removed, if necessary. The result of this is that if everything is done correctly the engine will be in perfect balance within the confines of four cylinder in-line design parameters.

The only way to check if an engine was balanced accurately by the factory is to rebalance the engine. Any engine that is going to be turned over 7000rpm on a continuous basis should be rebalanced. Any engine intended for racing must be rebalanced (to the last gram).

PISTON SETS

In practical terms ring sets are identical gram for gram in weight within a set of rings and usually within 0.07oz/2 grams manufacturer to manufacturer. Pistons are frequently within 0.035oz/1 gram within a set but, occasionally, one piston will be lighter or heavier than the rest by 0.07-0.10oz/2-3 grams. Piston pins are almost always within 0.035oz/1 gram within a set but may vary 0.07-0.10oz/2-3 grams and sometimes more manufacturer to manufacturer.

The pistons and piston pins are, in the first instance, weighed individually to ascertain which piston and which piston pin are the lightest at all). If the piston pins are identical diameter (piston pins are selectively fitted to pistons on the basis of size) ut different in weight, they can be swapped around to help equalize the overall combination weights before any lightening is carried out. Weigh each piston and piston pin together. Frequently, the combined weight of the piston, piston pin and rings will see each set with a total mismatch of 0.07-.10oz/2-3 grams only.

With the weight of the lightest piston or pistons known and any piston pin swapping done, metal can be removed to equalize the weights. If the amount of material required to be removed is minimal it can be taken from the piston pin bosses of the piston (some pistons have excess material here) or from inside the ends of the piston pin. Some pistons have machined-in registers for the machining of the outside diameter of the piston, and material can be taken from the sides of these without detriment to piston strength.

The total weights each piston, piston pin and rings set must be equal to within 0.035oz/1 gram and this may mean metal removal from several pistons or wrist pins or a combination of both. If there is a considerable amount of weight, such as 0.14oz/4 grams, to be removed, it can be very difficult to take this amount off the piston. In such a case, remove material from the inside of the wrist pin bore using a die grinder. Up to 0.14oz/4 grams, or slightly more, can be removed from a wrist pin if material is removed from both ends of the wrist pin.

CONNECTING RODS

The connecting rods are balanced end for end and weight for weight with weight being apportioned to the big end and the little end. All of the big ends must be within 1 gram of each other as must the small ends; if not they'll have to be altered. Frequently, connecting rods are within 2-3 grams as they come from the manufacturer.

The lightest little end becomes the standard to which the other little ends are matched. Likewise, the lightest big end becomes the standard to which the others are matched. When the work is completed the little ends and the big ends will all weigh the same and the connecting rods will all, as a consequence, be the same total weight (1 gram ideally and 2 grams maximum). If the connecting rods are not the same overall weight check the weights of the little and big ends again: there has to be an error somewhere.

CRANKSHAFT

Crankshafts are normally well balanced just as they come from the manufacturer, but there is sometimes a wide tolerance on the allowable amount of imbalance. Some manufacturers balance their crankshafts to very tight tolerances, and when their crankshafts are checked for balance they are virtually perfect. The only way to ascertain whether the crankshaft is balanced correctly, or not, is to rebalance it.

FLYWHEELS

Flywheels are normally well balanced. Flywheels can be lightened within limits and the most effective place for lightening is as far away from the centre as possible. The reason for this is that force times distance applies and removal of material nearest the starter gear has more effect on the acceleration factor of the engine than material removed nearer the flange. **Caution!** - Avoid thin sections (less than 0.312in/8mm) when turning material off a flywheel as flywheels that are weakened through lightening may disintegrate in service. How much weight you can actually remove will depend entirely on the original thickness of your flywheel but, usually, it will be in the range of 20% to 50% of the original weight.

Balance a new pressure plate on the flywheel. Rebalance any flywheel that has been lightened: the crankshaft is balanced first and then the flywheel is added. The pressure plate is then added to the flywheel and balanced. Always get a new pressure plate when an engine is going to be rebalanced because a new pressure plate will last a lot longer than a used one.

Note that pressure plates are often advertised as being perfectly balanced with no need to check them. There is no doubt that pressure plates are balanced when they are made, or rebalanced when they are remanufactured, but there is nothing to say that the dowel holes in the flywheel being used are absolutely concentric with the dowels on the balancing machine in the factory where the pressure plate is made. There is room for error here.

Chapter 10
Camshaft and lifters

In most high performance applications a new camshaft and lifter (tappet) set will be used. However, note that even new camshafts must be checked for overall straightness and base circle runout - especially 'hydraulic' (ie. designed to operate with hydraulic lifters) camshafts. Checking the camshaft and all its lobes carefully prior to installation means that, should there be any problems later in tuning the engine, the camshaft does not have to be removed to be checked for possible error, specifically lobe error.

New camshafts are always supplied with details of lift and duration (camshaft card or as listed in a catalogue). This information can be used to ascertain whether the camshaft is as it should be, or, if the camshaft is used, by how much it has worn. Camshafts are usually identifiable as they are stamped by the manufacturer or stamped by the regrinding company. Specifications are generally obtainable one way or another.

Camshaft lobe being measured 'heel' to 'toe.'

Measuring each lobe heel to toe and 90 degrees from that, across the approximate base circle diameter, and then deducting the base circle size, is the quickest way of obtaining a reasonably accurate lift measurement.

USED CAMSHAFTS

The usual problem with used camshafts is lobe wear as the lobes are under considerable pressure at full lift because of valve spring pressure.

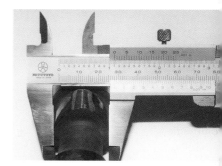

Camshaft lobe being measured across the base circle. This is not a dead accurate method, but it's reasonable, and certainly good enough to show a worn lobe.

When the lobes do start to wear the lift reduces, not only at full lift but the lift rate per degree of camshaft rotation is also usually down as the lobes wear back from the toe and down each side of the lobe. When lobes become worn the valve action gets very lazy and engine performance reduces as a consequence.

A further problem is that not all lobes wear at the same rate and, frequently, one or more lobes wear

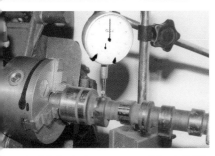

Camshaft lobe being measured for full lift. The dial indicator is shown set to zero on the 'heel' of the lobe.

The dial indicator is registering the full lift of this lobe.

xcessively in comparison to the other obes on the same camshaft. It only akes one lobe to be well down 0.060in/1.5mm, or more) and the amshaft is virtually a write off. Engine ower will also be down (lack of olumetric efficiency).

Lift wear is quite easy to check as ne base circle effectively remains 'on ize' (size as ground by the nanufacturer) and only the toe of the amshaft lobe reduces as it wears. A ernier caliper can be used to measure nis accurately enough.

Irrespective of the overall size of ne lobe, the actual wear that has aken place can be roughly scertained. The camshaft is placed etween lathe centres and a dial ndicator set to zero on the heel of ach camshaft lobe in turn. The lift is aken as the direct measurement from ne heel to the maximum attainable igh point of the toe. If the original obe height is known, it can be

compared with the measurement taken. Failing this, with the heel to toe dimension of each lobe known, each measurement is divided by the rocker arm ratio. This is then added to the heel to toe measurement and the resulting figure is the approximate camshaft lobe lift. The result is approximate because of production tolerances. Expect the lift to be less than advertised by the manufacturer, maybe by as much as 0.020in/0.50mm. This method can be used to check any lobe on any camshaft.

A used performance camshaft that is in good overall condition, apart from some wear, can always be sent back to the original grinding company and be reground with only the minimum amount of material being removed from it. The individual lobes will then all be freshly ground and to specification. It is far better to do this than to re-install a camshaft showing signs of wear and hope that what wear there is will not affect engine performance too much.

REGROUND CAMSHAFTS

Camshafts can be reground, but only if all lobes are still basically on size. Some wear is acceptable, but if one lobe is well down (0.060in/1.50mm, or more) the camshaft is not suitable for regrinding. If all of the lobes are very similar in size (within 0.005in/0.125mm, when measured from heel to toe and across base circle) then the camshaft will almost always take a regrind. The largest inlet lobe and the largest exhaust lobe are the standard against which all other lobes on the camshaft are measured.

Some camshafts are not able to take high lift performance grinds because the lobe is physically very small in relation to the core diameter of the camshaft. For the camshaft

A camshaft lobe that has been built up with a hard surfacing agent. The lobe can be easily ground back to size with a build up like this on it.

lobes to take a performance grind, too much material would have to be removed from the base circle of the camshaft lobe and this may mean that the core diameter of the camshaft gets undercut. **Caution!** - This is not desirable as the camshaft is weakened, especially if a sharp corner is formed: camshafts like this often break in service, causing serious damage. Such camshafts can be built up using a hard surfacing agent, but this is costly. One or two lobes can be repaired on a camshaft to restore them to original size using the same method. The alternative is a 'blank' camshaft.

A blank camshaft as made by, or for, one of the specialist camshaft manufacturers is basically a new camshaft with generous large lobe forms that will allow any camshaft profile to be put on them. These camshafts are frequently made with a slightly smaller core diameter and a lobe size that has a similar sized base circle as the original equipment camshaft (or as near as they can get it). The lift being much more than the original equipment camshaft will mean that there is very little (if any) material to come off the base circle to 'fit' the new profile on.

A good used 'wild' camshaft will

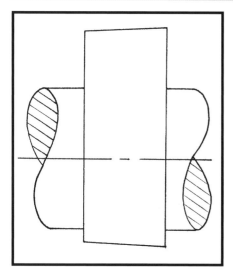

Diagram shows the taper found on all camshaft lobes.

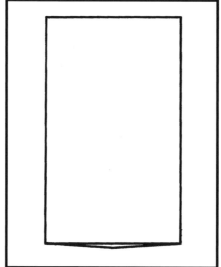

Diagram shows a lifter side on. The base of a lifter is convex.

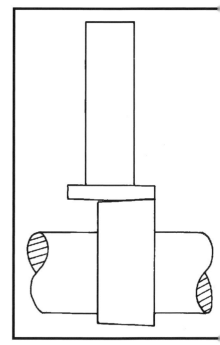

Diagram of a lifter and a camshaft lobe and the matching of the tapers on each when assembled in an engine.

take a regrind with a less radical grind with ease. The same checking criteria applies. The camshaft must be straight and have no excessively worn lobes (indicating soft lobes). If the camshaft has a damaged lobe, or lobes, the camshaft may still be able to be used, but only if the damage cleans up during the regrinding process.

There is nothing wrong with a camshaft regrind as long as the camshaft to be reground is straight, has polished journals (no pits or scores - which will cause camshaft bearing wear) and lobes that are stock and worn but otherwise on size. The regrind will be successful provided the lift required is not too much and there is no undercutting of the core.

LIFTERS

The base surface of a lifter wears concave after many miles and the surface may also begin to break up or become pitted. Once the surface of a lifter begins to break up it should not be reground as it is highly likely that the surface will continue to break up. Any new or reground camshaft **must** have lifters that are new, or lifters that are near new and have been refaced.

Lifters, when new or refaced, are not flat but slightly convex and, furthermore, camshaft lobes when new are also not level across the surface (parallel to the axis of the camshaft) but are tapered. Depending on engine design, the taper on the camshaft lobes of a particular camshaft can all slope one way or alternate from left to right, lobe to lobe. The taper on the camshaft lobe and the convex shape of the base of the lifter, plus the position of the lifter in relation to the camshaft lobe, promotes lifter rotation.

Lifters can be reground, but if they have done a lot of miles they should all be replaced as a matter of course. The internal components of hydraulic lifters also wear out.

SUMMARY

Only use refaced near new, or new lifters.

Any used camshaft must have 'o size' lobes.

Check that the taper of each lobe is running the correct way (the high side is toward the periphery of the lifter seat). With the camshaft mounted in lathe centres, the direction of lobe taper can be checked with a dial indicator.

Check that the journals are polished with no surface roughness.

Check that the camshaft is 'dead straight.

Chapter 11
Crankshaft
- check fitting

All of the parts that are going into your new' high-performance engine **must** e crack-free, remachined correctly nd spotlessly clean. Clean hands, ools and working area are **essential** or assembly work.

With all the parts machined to size ey must all be 'check fitted' into an ssembly that is going to work ogether perfectly. Just because all of e parts have been very carefully emachined, it does not mean that the unning fit' is absolutely correct. The t usually is correct but it still requires hecking.

The engine block can be painted t this stage, but do **not** use a heat esistant paint and do **not** put on more an two covering coats (heat resistant aint keeps the heat in).

Use thread tape on threaded lugs and a retaining compound or ilicone sealer on all press-in plugs.

Fit all freeze plugs into the block. se sealer on the plugs and on the lock recesses so that both parts are well coated before the plug is fitted. Wipe the excess sealer off and fit the straps. Coat the strap retaining screw threads with a retaining compound (Loctite, or similar) before screwing them into their holes.

If the engine has press-in oil gallery plugs and they have not been converted to screw-in plugs, they must be 'locked' in place to ensure that they do not come out in service. The easiest way of ensuring that these plugs do not come loose is to stake the edges of the holes that the press in plugs go into. This never looks very nice, but does prevent the plugs from coming out, even if they work loose.

Caution! - Many high-performance engines retain the standard press-in oil gallery plugs and never have one come loose or fall out in service. However, the rigours of use in a high-performance engine can mean that a plug which is not staked (or, preferably, replaced by a threaded plug) can be dislodged which will almost certainly result in a great deal of engine damage.

CAMSHAFT INSTALLATION (IF IN BLOCK)

New camshafts and reground camshafts are precision ground items, but there are occasions when things go wrong during manufacture and the time to check the complete integrity of the camshaft is now. Irrespective of which company ground the camshaft, it **must** be checked using the procedure described in the previous chapter.

Check that the oil holes of the camshaft bearings line up with the oilways in the block. Check that any oil gallery that is behind the camshaft sprocket (when the sprocket is fitted) and is not able to be seen has its plug fitted. Check to see that the front camshaft bearing is recessed slightly from the block surface so that the bearing can in no way interfere with the thrust plate or the drive sprocket.

Check the surface finish of the camshaft bearing journals. They must have a surface finish just like that of a crankshaft journal because excessive journal roughness will cause cam bearing wear. High performance use will impose high loads on these bearings, especially when high valve spring pressures are used along with high rpm.

The camshaft is now carefully installed in the engine block to check that it turns freely without binding at any point.

The camshaft journals and the bearings must be oiled before the camshaft is installed into the block. Engine oil can be used, or one of the more specialized assembly oils such as Wynns Additif, or similar, which is excellent for all bearing assembly. Note that a specialized assembly oil such as this **must never** be used on piston rings: they will never seat.

The camshaft is the first component into the engine because it can be guided from bearing to bearing through the block quite easily when the crankshaft is out. **Caution!** - Take extreme care when feeding the camshaft through the block to ensure that the camshaft lobes do not come into contact with the bearing surfaces. The problem is that as the camshaft is being fed from bearing to bearing, its lobes can come into contact with the bearings and cause damage, especially when the camshaft bearing journal leaves a bearing and the camshaft is allowed to drop down.

Once the camshaft is installed, fit the thrust plate using the correct screws and then check the camshaft for free rotation. The camshaft **must** turn freely without any binding whatsoever. Fit the camshaft sprocket to the camshaft and fit the screws. Check that the screws are the right

ones and not too long which, if unnoticed, could foul the thrust plate or the block.

CRANKSHAFT INSTALLATION

Clean the bearing shells thoroughly with a solvent and wipe them with paper towels. Clean the block tunnels with solvent and wipe them with paper towels. Clean the bearing surfaces of the crankshaft. Bearing shells are fitted into the block tunnels dry (that is the backs of the bearing shells!)

Block shells **must** always have a groove in the surface for oil distribution to allow 180 degree oiling. The main cap bearing shells can be plain or they, too, can come with grooves in them for 360 degree oiling depending on engine design.

Check that all oil holes in the main bearing shells do, in fact, line up with the oil gallery holes as drilled in the block.

Thrust bearings

The majority of four cylinder engines have a centre main thrust bearing comprising two or four C-shaped thrust washers or a combination main and thrust washer bearing. Engines equipped with four C-shaped thrust washers seldom have crankshaft thrust bearing problems (high wear rate) while those engines equipped with two C-shaped thrust washers often have thrust washer wear problems even in standard form. **Caution!** - Engines equipped with only two C-shaped crankshaft thrust washers need frequent thrust washer changes if a heavy duty clutch cover assembly is fitted. To improve the longevity of this type of thrust bearing, avoid prolonged depression of the clutch pedal.

Before proceeding any further the crankshaft endfloat **must** be

Main bearing shell installed in engine block.

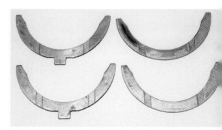

Plain shell fitted to main cap.

Set of four C-type thrust washers.

Combination main and thrust bearing.

measured. Endfloat is measured by fitting the bearing shell (combined thrust washer type) into the appropriate main bearing cap (usually the centre main), placing the cap on the appropriate crankshaft journal, pushing it to one side and then simply

Thrust bearing being checked for end clearance using a feeler gauge.

Combination main/thrust bearing fitted to the crankshaft with a feeler gauge being used to measure the gap. The clearance equals the amount of crankshaft endfloat.

Main cap, with both thrust washers fitted, being measured with an outside micrometer.

checking to see what size of feeler gauge fills the resulting gap between the thrust washer thrust face and the crankshaft thrust face.

With a C-type thrust washer arrangement, the endfloat is the

Telescopic gauge being used to measure the distance between the thrust surfaces of this crankshaft (outside micrometer is put over the gauge to get the measurement).

difference between the measurement taken over the main cap with both thrust washers in place and the distance between the two thrust faces of the crankshaft.

Whatever the endfloat measurement is, the same clearance **must** be found when the cap is installed in the engine and the crankshaft endfloat checked.

Caution! - If the crankshaft endfloat (when measured later in the build procedure) is smaller than the measurement taken now, something - most likely a main cap - is misaligned, maybe because of loose or undersized locating dowels.

Caution! - Note that while most of the clearances used for high performance engines are the maximum of the manufacturer's tolerances, crankshaft endfloat should be in the middle of the tolerance

range. Endfloat problems can be resolved with oversize thrust washers (combined with regrinding the crank's thrust faces or, ultimately, replacing the crankshaft.

'Check fitting' the crankshaft to the block

The crankshaft is now fitted into the block so that all bearings can be checked for binding. A part of this procedure is to double-check that the crankshaft is, in fact, straight. This involves fitting the crankshaft into the block with only the front and rear main bearings and caps fitted.

The centre main incorporates the thrust bearings and, as it won't be installed during this procedure, something must be done to prevent the crankshaft thrust surfaces contacting the block. The solution to this problem is to place tape over the main bearing web/main bearing register so that there is a buffer between the crankshaft's thrust faces and the block itself. The crankshaft is only going to be rotated by hand but any contact **must** be avoided. Racing (Duct) tape is ideal for this as it is quite sticky: most other sticky tapes do not adhere well to as-cast, cast iron or aluminium surfaces.

Clean the front and rear block tunnel surfaces and the backs of the front and rear main bearing shell inserts. Fit the front and rear bearing insert halves into the block and liberally coat the bearing surfaces with oil.

Oil the front and rear main journal surfaces and then carefully place the crankshaft into the block: **do not** turn the crankshaft.

Remove the bearing shells from the main caps, clean the backs of the shells with solvent and wipe them clean with paper towels. Clean the tunnel surfaces of the main caps with

Dial indicator spindle placed on the centre journal of this crankshaft. Note that this block has a centre thrust bearing, and that there is tape covering the thrust surfaces of the block.

Tape placed over each web of the centre main: it will act as a buffer for the crankshaft thrust bearing surfaces.

Thrust fitted to a cap. Note the two grooves in this C-type thrust.

solvent and wipe them clean with paper towels. This will mean that the backs of the bearing shells and the main cap tunnel bore surfaces are absolutely clean and the fit between the inserts and the block tunnel is as near metal to metal contact as possible.

Lubricate the bearing shell surfaces with engine oil/assembly lube and fit the two main caps to the block and torque the bolts/studs to the recommended torque. The crankshaft can now be turned without risk of damage.

Using a dial indicator and magnetic stand on a cast iron block, or a dial indicator and clamp on an alloy block, position the dial indicator spindle on one side of the journal (otherwise the dial indicator spindle may catch in the oil hole). Set the dial indicator needle to zero and then rotate the crankshaft slowly by hand

and check the crankshaft for runout. The crankshaft should have zero runout but it is permissible to have a maximum of 0.001in/0.028mm on the centre main. Anything more than this and the crankshaft is technically bent. If the dial indicator needle moves the crankshaft is bent or the journal is oval or has been incorrectly ground. **Caution!** - Do not proceed with the engine assembly until the reason for an error is known and any problem/s corrected.

If the crankshaft has three main bearings the checking is now complete. If the crankshaft has five main bearings the other two main bearing journals are checked in like manner using the same criteria.

With the crankshaft checked for straightness the two main caps are undone and removed and the crankshaft lifted out to remove the buffer tape.

Clean the remaining block tunnels using solvent and wipe them with paper towels. Check that grooved bearing shells are placed in the block and that the oil feed holes line up with the block's drilled holes. Clean the backs of the remaining bearings, wipe them clean using paper towels and install all bearings in the block.

Liberally coat the bearing shell surfaces, thrust washers and crankshaft journals with engine oil.

Oil can be used to 'stick' the thrust washers (C-shaped type) to the block before the crankshaft is fitted or the crankshaft can be rested in the block and the thrust washers slid into place. The important point is to avoid direct contact between the crankshaft and the block.

Caution! - C-shaped thrust washers **must** have the correct orientation, but it is possible to install them the wrong way around. The steel surface of the thrust washer **must** face the block and not the crankshaft. The thrust washer surface that faces the crankshaft has parallel oil grooves in it. Check this point thoroughly as thrust washers placed in an engine the wrong way around ruin the engine very quickly.

Liberally coat the main bearing journals with engine oil. Carefully lower the crankshaft into the block bearings: **do not** turn the crank.

Remove the bearing shells from the remaining main caps and clean the backs of the shells with solvent. Wipe them clean with paper towels and refit the shells to the main caps. Lubricate the bearing shell surfaces with engine oil. Position the main caps on to the block, fit the bolts and torque them to the recommended tension. The crankshaft can only be turned after all main caps have been torqued.

Crankshaft endfloat being measured with a feeler gauge.

A crankshaft installed in a block with one pair of bearing shells removed. If the binding is no longer there, this is the bearing combination causing the problem.

Front seal on the left and larger rear seal on the right.

Recess that takes the oil seal is machined into the cap and block. This engine has an extended skirt block.

This rear oil seal fits into a housing which is then bolted to the back of the block.

Check the endfloat of the crankshaft using the correct sized (true endfloat was measured earlier) feeler gauge (or, perhaps, 0.001in 0.02mm less) placed between the bearing thrust surface and the crankshaft. If there is less clearance than there should be, incorrectly seated thrust bearings/washers or misalignment of the cap carrying the thrust washers is indicated. Note that the main cap which houses the thrust bearing/washers is **always** positively located, usually by dowels, so its position should be correct unless the dowels have been removed and not replaced, or if the dowels are undersized and loose. **Caution!** - Find out why the correct endfloat is not there **before** proceeding with engine assembly.

With all bolts torqued to the recommended figures, check the crankshaft for freedom of rotation. The crankshaft should spin with a flick of the wrist and continue moving for a half turn, or more.

Caution! - The crankshaft must not be rotated until all of the bolts have been fully tensioned because, until the main caps are under tension, the bearing shells are not forced, by crush effect, to assume the true round shape of their tunnels. The bearing shells can be rubbed or suffer surface scuffing if the crank is rotated before the main caps are tensioned.

If the crankshaft is found to be binding, the offending bearing or bearings will have to be located. This is achieved in the first instance by undoing all main cap bolts and removing the crankshaft. Then wipe all of the oil off the bearing shells in the block and the caps with a paper towel. Check each shell for shiny scuff marks or rub marks. If, for instance, one pair of bearing shells is marked with a shiny spot, that is most likely the pair that is causing the problem.

To check whether or not a pair of bearing shells is actually binding, remove these two bearing shells from the block and cap. Oil the bearing shells again and install the crankshaft. Refit the main caps and 'snap' them into position and torque the bolts up. Once this is completed the pair of bearing shells will be out of the equation and, if the crankshaft is then able to turn freely, the problem bearing will have been located.

The majority of modern engines have 360 degree lip-type oil seals, which are installed in machine recess form in the block and rear main cap, or the seal is fitted into its own housing and bolted onto the rear of the block. These 360 degree lip-type oil seals press into the block recess or housing with a sealant on the outside diameter of the seal to prevent oil leaks. This type of seal is universally used on the rear main and crankshaft front.

Other systems of rear main oil seals, such as reverse screw threads and rope type seals, are used in older engine designs. Check with a specific workshop manual for individual fitting instructions. All systems work well if fitted correctly.

The usual 360 degree lip-type

one-piece oil seal does not cause any significant drag during crankshaft fitting and freedom of rotation testing, but the seal is not fitted until after the crankshaft has been 'check fitted' because the crankshaft may have to be fitted into the block two or three times.

There should not be any problems with the crankshaft installation because this is, in effect, the final assembly with the crankshaft journals and bearing bores having been measured previously. Any problems should have been found and sorted out earlier. The check fitting process is designed to pick up previously missed errors. **Caution!** - If there are problems of any description, remove the crankshaft and start again checking everything as you go. That is the main bearing tunnel bore diameters, the journal diameters and the bearing bores.

Chapter 12
Timing chain

The following applies to simplex or duplex timing chain driven, in-block camshafts. Most original equipment timing chains are simplex (single row) and are not suitable for high-performance engines. Sometimes there is no alternative but to use a simplex chain; if so, buy and fit the very best quality chain available. If a duplex chain drive is available, fit it! Whatever the chain type, **always** fit a new tensioner and rubbing blocks.

Note there are engines that have overhead camshafts (single or twin) driven by a single row chain. With such engines often a single row chain has to be used: the chains on these engines **must** be changed regularly in high-performance applications. Avoid using a long simplex chain on an overhead camshaft engine, if at all possible.

Basically, all chain types 'stretch' through component wear, but different designs and the quality of the individual components play a major

part in how well a particular chain will stand up in service. Inexpensive chains are frequently not able to take the stress of high-performance application (they are an absolute waste of time).

Chain sprockets are usually steel and quite satisfactory.

The majority of engines rebuilt for high-performance will be fitted with a replacement duplex roller timing chain and sprocket set, as such kits are readily available for most popular engines and are quite reasonable in price. These chains offer markedly

Twin row roller timing chain and sprockets.

increased durability over stock simplex timing chains because there are double the number of links and twice the pin area.

FITTING TIMING CHAINS

The bottom sprocket is fitted on to the crankshaft using a copper drift. The fit of the sprocket to the crankshaft may be quite tight through to being reasonably loose. It does not have to be very tight on the crankshaft snout because, once the front pulley is fitted and the crankshaft bolt fully done up, there is no possibility of any movement.

The sprocket's inside diameter can be eased if necessary but not the crankshaft snout as, in future, an alternative timing set may be used and the fit could then be very loose. The inside of the sprocket can be eased with a high speed die grinder with a flap wheel fitted which effectively

Camshaft sprocket and the bottom sprocket in alignment with the centres of the crankshaft and the camshaft.

The timing chain and sprockets forward of their final fitted position. Chain and sprockets will move back easily as a unit like this. Note that this would not be possible if the bottom sprocket was firmly fixed against the front journal in its normal fitted position.

Timing chain and sprockets in their final position. The sprocket marks are lined up but the camshaft timing could still be slightly out.

lightly polishes the bore until the fit is a true 'tap fit.'

Ideally the fit of the sprocket to crankshaft is a light tap-on fit and a light tap-off fit for removal (using a copper or aluminium drift). Sprockets that have been 'hammered on' are exceedingly difficult to remove. To avoid this situation, only fit the bottom sprocket if it can be tapped on using light blows. If, when tapping the sprocket on, the fit gets tighter, do not persist: remove the sprocket immediately and ease the inside diameter.

Temporarily fit the camshaft sprocket and then place the chain onto it with the chain angled forward slightly in front of the crankshaft sprocket. With the sprockets correctly lined up, mark the chain and sprockets with a felt tipped pen so that the chain can be correctly matched to either sprocket. Remove the chain and then the camshaft sprocket from the camshaft.

For ease of fitting of the timing chain and camshaft sprocket, move the bottom sprocket a good half inch/ 13mm forward (towards the front of the crankshaft snout) from the front bearing journal. The reason for this is

that, if the chain is very tight (desirable), it will be angled forward before it can be fitted to the camshaft and considerable force can be required to get the camshaft sprocket on to the camshaft. This can all be avoided if the chain and the two sprockets go back together on to the engine at a true 90 degrees to the crankshaft axis.

With the chain fitted to the camshaft sprocket and the felt tipped pen lines correctly lined up, offer the chain up to the crankshaft sprocket so that the felt tipped pen lines on the bottom sprocket and chain are also lined up. The sprockets are now in correct phasing and need only to be moved backwards onto the camshaft

and crankshaft.

Camshaft sprockets are located by dowel or keyway and then bolted on. Check that the sprocket dimples or arrows are in line with the central axis between the crankshaft centre line and the camshaft centre line.

CAMSHAFT TIMING

Normally the camshaft is installed in the engine and the two sprockets are lined up using the dimples or arrows and the timing gear marks are the only things used to time the camshaft. The camshaft timing could be anything from absolutely 'spot-on' to several degrees advanced or retarded: this is not acceptable for a high-performance engine. The engine may run well with unchecked camshaft timing but it's unlikely to give optimum power. Ther no guarantee that the camshaft is timed to the manufacturer's specifications or timed to give best power when only the dimples or arrows on the crankshaft sprocket and camshaft sprocket are used to set the engine: there are just too many variables.

Correct camshaft timing is a **vital** part of engine tuning and it **must** be checked and adjusted if necessary.

There are several variables that must be taken into account when considering the drive from the crankshaft to the camshaft. The timing chain may not be tight when fitted to the engine, the key in the front of the crankshaft may be slightly out of position (advanced or retarded), the camshaft sprocket may not be dowelled or keyed in position correctly (advanced or retarded), or the keyway in the bottom sprocket may not be accurate (advanced or retarded).

Accurate valve timing

This involves setting the camshaft in relation to the crankshaft so that, by whatever means of adjustment there is, the inlet valve of number one cylinder is in the full lift position at the camshaft manufacturer's prescribed number of degrees.

The full lift position is the ideal point to set the camshaft timing to, because it is reasonably easy to check repeatedly. The actual degree marking has to be accurately marked onto the crankshaft pulley after a dial indicator is used to accurately pinpoint the full lift position of the lifter. Note that the lifter and bore is not oiled for the timing check and that light downward finger pressure on the lifter may be necessary to ensure that it follows the camshaft lobe after full lift has been reached.

The engine is only turned one way when the timing is being checked (clockwise). In the first instance the full lift position is found and the dial indicator set to zero. The engine can now be turned back to at least 30 degrees and then bought back to 0.010in/0.25mm of the dial indicator's zero mark. Stop rotating the crankshaft

at this point and mark the damper using a white fine nib felt tipped pen on the rim of the damper adjacent to the TDC pointer. Continue to rotate the crankshaft till the zero mark comes up on the dial indicator and go on rotating the crankshaft until the dial indicator needle registers the 0.010in or 0.25mm position again. Mark the rim of the crankshaft damper adjacent to the TDC marker with the felt tipped pen once again. The degree marking for full lift on the rim of the damper should be exactly in the middle of the two white felt tipped pen lines just drawn on to the rim of the damper.

With timing chains the timing should be advanced by 1 degree as, when the engine is fully built up, the valve springs will load the camshaft and cause the chain to be under tension, similar to when the engine is in operation. Recheck the camshaft timing after the engine is fully assembled just to be sure that the camshaft timing matches the camshaft manufacturer's degree setting for full lift or 1 degree advance of this.

Chapter 13
Valve reliefs & fitting pistons to connecting rods

PISTON VALVE RELIEFS

Some pistons have valve reliefs in their crowns to provide working clearance for the valves. Most engines have plenty of clearance for the working relationship between pistons and valves, but many engines do not have clearance for the valves through full crankshaft rotation when the camshaft/s and crankshaft are not connected by the timing chain/belt - this is particularly true of modern multi-valve engines.

This means that, on many engines, if the valves are in the fully opened position and the engine is turned (camshaft/s disconnected), the valves get bent. The working relationship between pistons and valves needs to be addressed before the engine is assembled.

Heads get planed, blocks get planed and camshafts get changed, all of which reduce from standard the amount of piston to valve clearance.

On most multi-valve engines, for example, it is impossible to prevent piston to valve collision when camshaft timing is wrong or chain/belt failure occurs.

The idea of having as much piston to valve clearance as possible in the interests of reliability is well founded but, in most cases, the fact that valves can still get bent in certain situations has to be accepted.

On a vertical valve engine which has the combustion chamber in the cylinder, for instance, there may well be 0.400in/10.0mm piston to valve clearance when the engine is at TDC on the firing stroke. Such engines often have 100% rotational clearance even if the timing chain breaks. After the block of such an engine has been planed, the head planed and the camshaft changed, the engine may well still have 0.275in/7.0mm piston to valve clearance at TDC firing. The only way that piston to valve contact can occur is in an extreme over-

revving situation and, even then, only the exhaust valves will be bent.

On modern four valve per cylinder engines, the trend is to use fl topped pistons, with the piston crown 0.020in/ 0.5mm below the block deck at TDC, a thick head gasket (0.065in. 1.65mm) and a cylinder head design which has as much distance as possible between the bottom edge of the valves and the cylinder head face This design allows good piston to valve clearance and is good for emissions. In such cases the pistons usually have valve reliefs machined ir them, even if the depth is only 0.125in/3.2mm to 0.187in/4.8mm.

In an ideal situation there is a minimum of 0.100in/2.5mm piston to valve clearance.

Once the pistons have been individualized to a particular cylinder, the existing valve reliefs can be deepened and have their diameters increased (if the valve size is to be enlarged). If the block deck or cylinde

VALVE RELIEFS & FITTING PISTONS TO CONNECTING RODS

...ead has been planed to increase ...ompression ratio, the piston to valve ...learance will have been reduced and ...e valve reliefs will have to be ...eepened just to restore the original ...iston to valve clearance. Further to ...is, if the camshaft duration is ...icreased the valves will be opening ...arlier and will get closer to the piston ...rown than with a stock camshaft ...tted, and higher lift will exacerbate ...e problem. **Caution!** - The valve ...eliefs **must** be increased in depth to ...ompensate for planing of the block or ...ead and the increase in camshaft ...uration and lift.

Note that inlet valves are closest ... the piston at TDC (opening) and ...fterward for 2 to 3 degrees. The ...xhaust valves are closest to the piston ...ist before TDC (closing). The inlet ...alve begins to open BTDC (before ...op dead centre) and continues to ...pen at the lift rate of the camshaft. ...he piston comes up to TDC and ...ops momentarily and then begins to ...iove away from TDC, accelerating as ... goes. The valve, on the other hand, ...s lifting and it is just before TDC, at ...DC or slightly after TDC, that the ...alve can collide with the piston crown ... there is insufficient piston to valve ...earance. The exhaust valve is closing ...s the piston is rising to TDC and if ...iere is insufficient piston to valve ...earance the piston will hit the valve ...TDC (before top dead centre). The ...iston will not collide with the valve ...ter TDC because the valve is ...ontinuing to close at TDC and after.

The piston to valve clearance ...eeds to be as great as possible within ...ie confines of the piston crown ...iickness. **Caution!** - Valve reliefs ...ust not be deepened to the point ...here the crown becomes too thin for ...liability. The minimum crown ...ickness at the deepest part of the ...lve relief has to be 0.187in/4.8mm.

Accurate valve relief location

It is **vital** that the valve relief is on centre with the axis of the valve. The best method of accurately finding the position of the valves on any engine is to spot through a cylinder head valve guide bore (head gasket in place) onto the piston crown with each piston at TDC.

The engine will have to have the pistons fitted to the connecting rods so that the connecting rods and pistons can be installed temporarily in the block. Undersize (by 0.003in/0.075mm) dummy piston pins will have to be made up (aluminium is okay) for this purpose. Temporarily install each piston/connecting rod assembly in its designated cylinder and fit the shells and rod caps. **Caution!** - place lengths of flexible fuel pipe over protruding con rod bolts to protect the

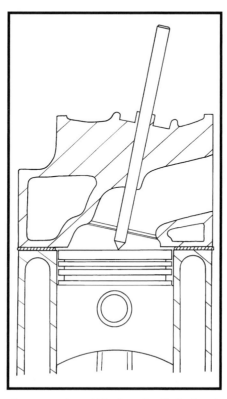

Cross section of block and cylinder head showing a long spotting punch in use.

crankshaft journals when fitting the rod/piston assemblies.

Next, the bare cylinder head is fitted to the block and the centre of each valve guide transferred to the top of each piston crown at TDC using a long spotting punch of the same diameter as the valve stems that is fitted down through the valve guide. Most cylinder heads are located on dowels, but not all, and there is often some movement on such heads as the studs or bolts only are used to locate the cylinder head. In such cases push the cylinder head to one side before tightening it, spot the valve guide centres on that side of the engine, then loosen off the studs or bolts and push the cylinder head to the other side of the engine. Tighten the studs or bolts again and spot the valve guide centres of that side.

Valve relief diameters

The diameter of the valve relief as cut into the top of the piston needs to be 0.040in/1.0mm more than the actual valve diameter. If the diameter of the relief is made too large the effective

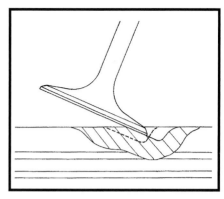

Cross section of a piston crown illustrates the effect of a valve relief in the wrong position or one with to large a diameter. If in the wrong position, although theoretically deep enough, the valve will contact the piston. If the diameter is too large, the potential depth is reduced because the unused area is at the deepest point.

depth of the piston to valve clearance will be considerably reduced. The valve relief will look quite large and be to the maximum depth possible but, in actual fact, will be reducing compression and not giving the maximum amount of piston to valve clearance possible. Such a relief might look very good but will not be very effective.

Caution! - Valve reliefs do lower the compression to a certain degree, but on **no account** should the valve reliefs not be deepened in order to keep compression up. The reliability of the engine is far more important than the resulting slight loss of compression. Many an engine has been ruined through insufficient piston to valve clearance because engine compression was regarded as more important.

The valve centre dots on the top of each piston are used to swing engineer's dividers. The dividers will have been set to the valve diameter plus the clearance allowance. This gives a good visual guide to the finished relief size but the line is not 100% accurate as the piston top is not at the same angle as the valve.

If the pistons are then set up on a milling machine the valve reliefs can be cut to suit any valve size and any depth (within the bounds of piston crown thickness). The piston is held at an appropriate angle (spindle axis of the milling machine vertical) and the fly cutter used to take a series of 0.010in/0.025mm cuts until the required depth is reached. Many of the better-equipped engine machine shops have a special fixture for the universal machining of any automotive piston crown, irrespective of the valve angles involved. These fixtures hold the piston firmly and there is no possibility of it coming loose. The centre pop mark is used to set the milling table travel. This way the dial on the

machine can be set on zero and run up to that mark each time the table is traversed. The increased depth of the valve relief is measured on the first piston machined and the table wound up to a specific point on the dial for each piston. This process is accurate to within 0.008in/0.2mm, or so. The fly cutter's cutting edge must not be a sharp cornered cutting tool, there must be a 0.015in/0.4mm radius on it. Sharp corners can be a starting place for cracks! Remove sharp edges from the tops of the reliefs, too.

Wash the pistons thoroughly after machining to remove all swarf and blow them dry and clean with compressed air (**Warning!** - wear protective goggles).

FITTING PISTONS TO CONNECTING RODS

Interference fit piston pins
The pistons and connecting rods are put together using a machine designed for this very purpose. The machine has an induction heater which heats the small end of the connecting rod within strictly controlled limits; there is no possibility of the connecting rod being overheated. The wrist pin is pushed through the connecting rod and into the other side of the piston to a set depth, which means that the connecting rod is accurately centralized. **You are strongly advised to use this method of assembly.**

Because the engine has had dummy assemblies, the various components are not able to be mixed up: everything has been carefully numbered so there should be no assembly mistakes. If there are, and a piston is put on the wrong way around, the wrist pin will have to be pressed out again. There is some risk of damage to the piston when this is

Special machine used to assemble new pistons to connecting rods. Find an engine machine shop that has one of these machines and get them to do the work.

done. Double-check the relationship of each piston and connecting rod **before** assembly to avoid any mistakes.

There are other assembly methods. One alternative involves heating the small end of the connecting rod using a propane torch but there is the risk of the connecting rod being overheated. Over a certain

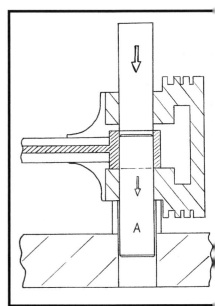

Mandrel ('A') in position on the lower side of the piston. Note that the mandrel is perfectly locating the connecting rod in the same axis.

temperature the connecting rod material (a premium grade of high tensile steel) will lose the ability to hold the wrist pin correctly (loses material strength). Any connecting rod that has been overheated (1200 degrees F/650 degrees C) can be considered no longer serviceable: the connecting rod has been heated until it is bright red or more. The difficulty with this method is the lack of control over the heating process and the problem of how to achieve correct wrist pin positioning before the heat transfers and locks the connecting rod and wrist pin together.

Another method involves pressing the wrist pin through the piston and connecting rod small end. The potential problem with this method is the amount of force required to press the pin in and the damage to the side of the piston which is being pressed against that this makes possible. Experience with this assembly method precludes problems.

If this method is used the piston pin must be lined up with the piston's piston pin bore using a dummy piston pin of almost the same diameter as the wrist pin. The dummy pin is a finger push fit into the piston and connecting rod small end to avoid 'galling' the inside of the connecting rod and damage to the new piston's piston pin bore.

The dummy pin locates in one side of the piston's piston pin bore and in the connecting rod, while the real piston pin is pressed in from the other side of the piston, displacing the dummy as it goes.

Although with this method the new piston pin is pressed through the connecting rod with the certainty that the connecting rod is 100% in line, the amount of pressure used to press the piston pin into the connecting rod could result in some 'galling' of the connecting rod small end bore and

particles going into the piston bore and distortion of the piston. Another problem with this method is that you may not know that something has gone wrong!

Some engine machine shops will have pressing equipment and mandrels that have been specifically made for the pistons you are using. This way the piston is correctly supported when it is being pressed against the base adapter and the connecting rod is located in line with the wrist pin bore in the piston.

An experienced operator can fit pistons and connecting rods correctly with the right gear. It is when the assembly jigs are not quite right that there is the potential for serious assembly problems which could result in engine damage.

Note that connecting rods should always have old pistons pressed off without any form of heating being applied to the connecting rod to shift the wrist pin. **Caution!** - Discard any connecting rod that looks like it has been grossly overheated and has a distorted small end (oval).

Connecting rods can be hardness tested. The connecting rod can be checked for hardness on the 'I' beam and then tested on the small end of the rod for a direct comparison. An overheated small end will be well down on hardness (usually measured with a Rockwell hardness tester using the C scale). This test settles any doubt as to the integrity of the material strength of the connecting rod.

With the pistons and connecting rods assembled, check the wrist pins for freedom of movement in the piston bores. With a small amount of oil on the wrist pin, the connecting rod should be absolutely free to move. **Caution!** - Do not let the connecting rod slap hard against the piston skirts!

Each connecting rod and piston

must now be checked for correct alignment. When the connecting rods were being prepared they were checked for straightness in both planes on a connecting rod alignment jig. This jig has an additional fixture that allows the connecting rod and piston to be checked when assembled. So, although the connecting rods have been checked and are known to be correct the pistons have not been checked but can now be via this means.

The connecting rod and piston is placed on the jig with a view to checking the working relationship. If any piston/connecting rod combination proves to be out, the piston is the problem. Once again this is the best method of checking these components as the parts are assembled just as they will be within the engine. The alignment of the piston and connecting rod must be within 0.0005-0.001in/0.013mm-0.025mm. Pistons are very accurately machined but, occasionally, one will be 'out' and the time to find it is now **before** it is installed in the engine. Check each piston and connecting rod.

Circlip retained piston pins

Ensure the piston is the right way round and is the correct piston before sliding in the piston pin. Note that to aid assembly the piston can be heated with a propane torch to the point when the piston is hot but can still be handled. The stamped steel circlips are the easiest to install as they have eyes to locate circlip pliers. These circlips are installed with the sharp edge facing the side of the piston and the rounded edge facing the end of the piston pin.

<u>Caution!</u> - Do **not** use stamped steel circlips more than once - and that means **one fitting**. Any suspected

Circlip being installed in piston pin bore.
Squeeze the circlip *just* enough to insert it
into the piston pin bore.

Circlip on the left has a sharp edge and
the circlip on the right has a rounded
edge.

deformation of the circlip caused by
squeezing it too much means that the
circlip is not serviceable. To check for
deformation place the circlip up
against another circlip that has not
been squeezed.

Some circlips of this type are
stronger than others. The ones shown
in the photograph are of average
strength on the basis of their
proportions. Using this sort of circlip
for piston pin retention is alright for
moderate peformance engines (not
highly loaded) and rpm up to 7000-
7500 when the pistons are new.
However, regular inspection of the
circlips and the grooves in the pistons
is recommended. Engines using these
circlips must have the minimum
amount of endfloat on the crankshaft,

medium bearing clearances, straight
connecting rods, 0.040in/1.0mm side
clearance between connecting rod little
end and piston bosses.

Once the circlip grooves show
signs of wear (new circlips are easy to
turn in the groove) it is time to replace
the pistons or use a different retention
method (Teflon buttons, for instance).
Not the most trustworthy piston pin
retention method to use on a well
modifed engine.

Round wire circlips are the most
difficult to fit (also they don't come out
very easily which is a good point, and
why they are used), especially the
thicker diameter wire ones (0.070in/
1.80mm). There is really no easy way
to fit strong round wire circlips without
the aid of a jig. The usual diameter of
round wire circlips is 0.050-0.060in/
1.27mm-1.52mm which represents a
considerable reduction in tension as
compared to the thicker ones. These
circlips can be inserted using the
following technique, which does
involve having some special parts
turned up to suit the particular piston
and piston pin.

The process involves making up a
tube that has an inside diameter the
same as the bore diameter of the
piston at one end, and which tapers
out (about 1 or 2 degrees) to the
diameter of the piston pin and the
diameter of the wire. There must be a
parallel section of at least 0.5in/12mm
leading up to the piston pin bore as
this is used to locate the pin used to
push the circlip into the piston pin
bore groove. This means that if the
piston pin is 0.945in/24mm in
diameter and the circlip 0.060in/
1.5mm, the outer diameter is 1in/
25.5mm. The amount of taper is not
critical and, as long the taper is not too
severe, the circlip will compress with a
minimum of effort as it is moved into
the tube by the push pin.

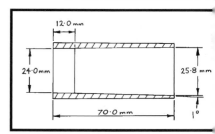

Special tube used to fit round wire
circlips.

The circlip will have to be
squeezed down to this diameter by
hand but this is relatively easy. The
other advantage of fitting cirlips usin
this method is that the circlip is only
squeezed as much as is absolutely
necessary.

There is some variation in the
machining of pistons that are designe
to use this sort of circlip, which does
lead to some complication. Some hav
a recess that leads into the piston pin
bore, while others are flat-sided (no
recess). Pistons with no machined
recess offer no way of lining up the
circlip accurately with the piston pin
bore. The tube must butt right up to
the side of the piston and be in perfe
alignment with the piston pin bore to
form a continuous bore from the tub
into the piston, otherwise the circlip
will spring out and not enter the actu
piston pin bore.

The solution to this problem is to
use a guide pin. This pin (custom
made) locates into the bore of the
piston pin and also in the bore of the
push pin (an old piston pin with a
squared-off end is ideal). This way th
alignment of the circlip is assured.

Oil the piston pin bore and the
bore of the tube and then install the
circlip into the tube. Using the push
pin, push the circlip into the bore of
the tube. The further the circlip is
pressed into the bore of the tube the
tighter it will get and more resistance
will be felt. Once the circlip reaches

A piston with a machined recess.

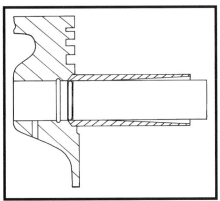

A circlip being installed using the tube method.

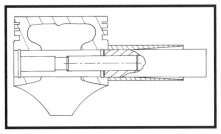

This piston has no recess. An extra guide pin is used to locate in the piston pin bore and also in the push pin's bore.

Correct position of circlip when fitted.

the parallel section of the tube the circlip will follow the end of the push pin (it will proceed along the parallel part of the tube at 90 degrees to the pin axis). **Warning!** - Once the circlip gets near to the end of the tube, slow down on the pushing as, if pressed too far, it will spring out with plenty of force and could be dangerous to you. To avoid losing the circlip, place the tube face down on to a flat solid surface and tap the push pin down until the circlip is in contact with the flat solid surface.

Warning! - Use safety glasses when carrying out the following operation to avoid possible eye injury and make sure that anyone else nearby is also wearing safety glasses. With the circlip in this position the tube can be placed in the machined recess of the piston or, if the piston has no recess, the guide pin fitted to the piston pin and the push pin located on the part of the guide that sticks out.

The connecting rod and piston are held in a vice for this procedure:

more specifically, the connecting rod is held in the vice across the big end of the connecting rod. Alternatively, the I-beam of the connecting rod can be held firmly between two pieces of wood (2in by 1in/50mm by 25mm) just below the skirt of the piston. This method tends to be firmer. Use jaw protectors to avoid any damage to the sides surfaces of the connecting rod. The tube is then inserted into the piston pin bore or located by the guide pin and pressure applied to the tube to move the piston over on the piston pin to stop all possible movement in that direction. The tube is held firmly against the piston and, using a small hammer, the push pin is tapped. The circlip is then moved on and into the tube and into the piston pin bore. The taps with the hammer obviously do not need to be heavy, just sufficient to move the circlip quickly. Speed of movement by the circlip into the piston pin bore is what is required for successful circlip fitting.

The openings of the circlips (irrespective of type) do not really have to be placed in any particular

position, but the generally accepted position is at 6 O'clock. If all circlips in the engine are placed in this position, any found to be in a different position when the engine is stripped at a later date, means that they have moved. The very strong round wire circlips do not tend to move at all but the stamped steel ones are prone to, especially if the piston pin has a lot of side load. The stamped steel circlip is not as strong as the round wire type and does not have as much surface contact area as a round wire circlip (perfectly round section in a perfectly machined groove).

The pistons and rods are now ready to be fitted to the engine block. Keep the pistons and connecting rods covered so that they are kept clean. Store them in clean plastic bags.

Chapter 14
Pistons & connecting rods - installation

At this point the pistons have been fitted to the connecting rods and can now be installed in the engine block.

PISTON RINGS

Measuring end gaps

Firstly, **all** (including oil control) piston rings are, in turn, fitted into the bore in which they will operate and the size of the ring gap checked with feeler gauges. For new bores, or on-size used bores, the rings are positioned approximately 0.125in/3mm down from the block deck. At this distance it is reasonably easy to see that the rings are square (ring surface parallel to block deck) in the bore. **Caution!** - If the ring is not square in the bore the ring could end up with insufficient gap because of an innacurate reading.

Alternatively, to ensure squareness, an upside-down piston can be used to push the ring at least 3in/75mm down the bore.

If the bores are even slightly worn

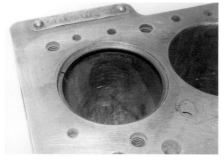
Ring positioned in the bore about 1/8in/ 3mm down from the block's deck. Bore has to be perfectly parallel if the gap is to be measured this way (as-new condition).

(0.002in/0.05mm maximum) the rings should be positioned at the bottom of the bore where virtually no wear is present. There is, however, no substitute for a bore being perfectly round and parallel: consider 0.002in/ 0.05mm the maximum amount of taper permissible. The reason for this is that the ring is effectively adjusting to a changing bore diameter every time the piston goes up and down in the cylinder. The ring gap at the

Inverted piston used to push ring square into bore.

bottom of the stroke might well be correct at, say, 0.010in/0.254mm but at the top of a 0.002in/0.050mm

pered bore, the gap will be 0.015in/
.38mm.

Optimum ring gaps vary
epending on the size of the piston.
he following table gives ring end gaps
or the top two compression rings for a
ange of piston diameters. Gaps **must**
ot be more than 0.004in/0.10mm
ver the recommended sizes. Because
ie table does not cover all individual
iston sizes, if the size of your pistons
not here, use the next size up.

74.0mm/2.914in piston - 0.010in/
.26mm gap.
80.0mm/3.150in piston - 0.012in/
.30mm gap.
86.0mm/3.385in piston - 0.014in/
.36mm gap.
92.0mm/3.625in piston - 0.016in/
.41mm gap.

Note that the second compression
ing can have a slightly smaller ring
nd gap without detriment because it
subjected to less heat and the
nallest useable ring gap is always
esirable. Second compression ring
aps are listed in the following table: if
ie size of your pistons is not here, use
ie next size up.

74.0mm/2.914in piston - 0.008in/
.20mm gap.
80.0mm/3.150in piston - 0.010in/
.26mm gap.
86.0mm/3.385in piston - 0.012in/
.30mm gap.
92.0mm/3.625in piston - 0.014in/
.36mm gap.

Oil control rings are less critical
neaning wider gaps are acceptable)
nd will frequently be found to have
aps of between 0.016-0.026in/0.31-
.75mm. A 74.0mm/2.914in piston
as an ideal oil ring end gap of
012in/0.31mm and a 92.0mm/
625in piston 0.016in/0.41mm. If an

oil ring set has large end gaps of
0.030-0.040in/0.72mm-1.0mm, install
them as they will still work correctly.
Oil rings seldom need to have material
removed to achieve the correct end
gap.

Altering ring gaps

If a ring has a gap that is smaller than
the minimum recommended size, it
must be eased. **Caution!** - End gaps
that are too tight can cause major
engine failure, so never take any ring's
end gap for granted; check each and
every one individually.

When gaps are set by the
manufacturer they are square, so that
if the ring is squeezed until the ends
butt there will be little, if any,
perceptible error as the two gap faces
meet. Rings with square end gaps are
correct.

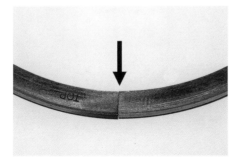

**Compression ring squeezed up so that the
ends butt up to one another. There is no
gap visible, which is correct.**

Ring end gaps can be hand filed
using needle files or any reasonably
small fine file. There is a certain
amount of dexterity required to hand
file the ends of rings, but it can be
carried out quite satisfactorily if care is
taken. In most instances ring gaps are
correct and require no remedial
rework.

There are hand operated ring
filers available and these devices are
excellent as both ends of the ring are
filed simultaneously and are dead
square when finished. This is the ideal

way to remove material from the ends
of the rings.

Side clearance

When fitted in the piston ring groove
the rings must be able to rotate easily
around the piston. Brand new pistons
will have about 0.001in/0.02mm to,
perhaps, 0.002in/0.05mm of side
clearance.

**Ring fitted into the piston groove and then
the side clearance is measured with a
feeler gauge.**

The groove of the top
compression ring is the one that wears
the most. The second compression
ring groove and the oil control ring
groove virtually never wear much from
the original size, even after many
thousands of road miles.

For high performance use the
wear limit for the top compression
ring's side clearance is 0.0025in/
0.063mm which is not much. With
0.003in/0.076mm and above of side
clearance, the rings will no longer hold
pressure correctly and 'blow by' into
the crankcase is the result. The only
real solution to this problem is to fit
new pistons.

Radial depth of the ring groove

The rings **must** fit **fully** into the groove
of the piston. It is usual for the ring to
fit flush with the ring lands of the

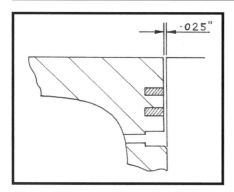

Ring fitted into the groove at full depth. Note that the edge of the ring that contacts the bore is flush with the side of the ring lands. This means that when the piston and ring are installed in the bore there is a gap of approximately 0.020in/ 0.50mm between the ring and the back of the piston groove.

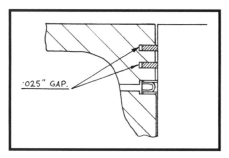

Working clearance between the back of the ring and the back edge of the ring groove in the piston.

piston when the ring is pressed into the groove by hand. A problem can arise when the rings are not the right ones for the piston set. **Caution!** - The radial depth of each ring must be checked.

With the end gaps, side clearance and groove depth all checked and correct, the rings can be fitted to the pistons.

FITTING RINGS TO PISTONS

Note that for ease of ring fitting, the connecting rod can be clamped in a vice (using soft jaws or jaw protectors).

Piston and connecting rod clamped in a vice which allows minimal piston movement and no possibility of damage to components.

Oil control rings

The first rings on to the piston are the oil control rings. The expander is placed into the groove first and the ends checked to make sure they are butting and not overlapping.

The end of a rail is then placed into the bottom of the groove 90 degrees around from the butted ends of the expander, and wound around the piston until all of the ring is positioned in the groove. Oil ring rails are quite resilient and can stand being distorted in this way to facilitate fitting.

With one rail fully fitted into the groove and correctly in contact with the expander, the ends of the expander can be clearly seen. If the expander's ends have become overlapped, lift the ring out of the groove and on to the ring land of the piston, line the ends up correctly and repeat the fitting procedure. Check the end of the expander again.

With one rail positively located in

Oil ring rail showing the end positioned i the groove and the rest of the rail about be wound around the piston lands and into the ring groove.

the groove and the expanders ends proved to be butted, the second oil ra can be fitted in the same manner as the first. With both rings fitted, the gaps of the rings are moved so that they are 180 degrees apart and the ends of the expander are 90 degrees away from either end of the oil rails.

With the gaps of the rails and the expander in the right position, the completed assembly is rotated aroun in the groove until the end gaps of th two rails are about 1in/25mm away from the piston pin.

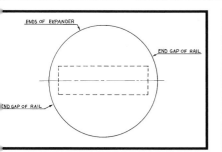

il control ring: the correct position of the nd gaps of the two rails and the expander in relation to the rails. The piston pin is also dotted in to show its position in relation to the end gaps of the rails.

Compression rings

se a ring expander to fit the two ompression rings to the pistons as this ill prevent ring breakage. A ring xpander spreads the ring evenly and so just enough for it to pass over the iston.

If the ambient temperature is very w (below 10 degrees C/50 degrees) the rings can be heated in a omestic oven to 70 degrees C/158 egrees F and fitted while still warm. hether this procedure is really ecessary depends on what the ring is ade of, but it's a good precaution gainst ring breakage.

Fit the second compression ring the piston first. Check that the ring the right way up according to the

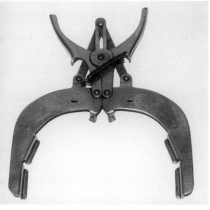

Piston ring expander for fitting rings to pistons without damage.

Compression ring being fitted on to a piston.

fitting instructions that come in the ring set package. The compression rings could have a dimple or lettering such as 'TOP' to indicate the right way up for the ring.

The top compression ring is fitted in the same manner as the second ring. With both compression rings fitted, rotate both in their respective grooves just to check for freedom of movement. At this point the pistons are ready to be fitted to the bores.

Just prior to installing a piston in its bore, and after the rings have been oiled, the ring gaps must be positioned. There are four end gaps to consider.

With the crankshaft big end journal of the cylinder having the piston fitted placed at bottom dead centre, the connecting rod can be fitted into the bore.

The connecting rod bolts must have connecting rod bolt guides fitted to them (short lengths of plastic fuel pipe are excellent for this) to protect the crankshaft journal from damage through contact with the threads of the bolts and also as a guide for ease of assembly. **Caution!** - Thread protectors or connecting rod bolt guides are essential for the protection of the crankshaft journal when connecting rods are fitted or removed from the engine.

The positions of all of the ring end gaps are checked (see diagram) before the ring compressor is fitted. It is often helpful if the connecting rod is held in

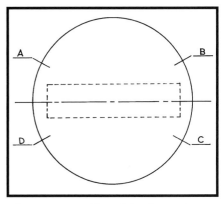

The correct position of the ring end gaps in relation to the wrist pin (looking at the top of a piston). A) top ring; B) bottom oil ring rail; C) 2nd compression ring; D) top oil ring rail.

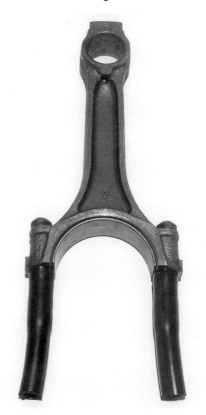

Thread protection (fuel hose) fitted to the bolts of a connecting rod.

When the connecting rod uses bolts only for cap retention, use temporary studs with chamfered ends to guide the connecting rod over the journal.

a vice (protectors fitted to the jaws) while the compressor is positioned. Apply plenty of straight 30/40 engine oil to the inside walls of the ring compressor. With the piston skirt and rings oiled sufficiently, the ring compressor is placed over the piston and clamping pressure applied.

Wipe the bore using a clean paper towel and then oil the bore with engine oil. This is best achieved by liberally applying oil to the bore with an oil can and smearing the oil over the surface of the bore with your fingers. **Caution!** - Absolute cleanliness is vital to avoid dirt particles being included in the assembly process. Use straight 30/40 engine oil to lubricate the pistons and rings. **Caution!** - Oiling pistons and rings with a friction modified oil and then using that same oil in the newly built engine frequently results in a smoking engine and poor ring sealing - so don't use it. The only solution to this problem is to strip the engine and replace the rings.

Wipe the crankshaft journal clean with a paper towel and then oil the surface. Use engine oil or an assembly lubricating oil (Wynns Additif or similar) and smear the oil over the

journal surface by hand. Check that the bearing shell is correctly positioned in the connecting rod, wipe the surface of the bearing shell with a paper towel and then oil the bearing surface.

With all surfaces cleaned and freshly oiled, check the forward facing position of the piston and then insert the connecting rod into the bore.

Note that if the engine block is on

Ring compressor.

Connecting rod held in a vice with the ring compressor fitted to it clamped up ready for fitting into the bore.

an engine stand, the block can be rotated until the bores are in the vertical plane and the relevant crankshaft journal positioned at bottom dead centre. This will ensure that the connecting rod hangs straight down and straddles the journal, but it will still need to be guided on to the journal by hand.

With the base of the piston fitted into the bore and the ring compressor's edge flush with the block's deck, the crown of the piston then tapped with the base of a hammer handle. The piston should slide into the bore with a minimum of resistance. If the piston is moving into the bore smoothly with each tapping motion and then stops moving and the next tap is accompanied by a firmer sound, stop tapping. Withdraw the piston, remove the ring compressor and check the oil control ring and, in particular, the butted ends of the expander. The usual cause of this scenario is that the oil control ring rail

Piston being tapped into the bore using the base of a hammer handle. No damage will be sustained by the piston crown.

as sprung out from under the compressor and is now no longer in line with the bore or, because of incorrect butting of the expander, that part of the oil ring rail is already past the bore perimeter. The situation requires refitting of the components and trying again. The piston and connecting rod assembly should move into the bore reasonably easily with no excessive force being necessary.

With the piston moving into the bore smoothly check the crankcase to see exactly where the bottom of the connecting rod is. Ideally the connecting rod will be lined up with and approaching the journal. If the connecting rod has turned slightly, straighten it up and then continue tapping the piston into the bore. Check the connecting rod's position regularly to make sure that it does approach the journal square on.

Once the piston crown has gone past the block's deck, the ring compressor is no longer needed and one hand can be used to hold on to the thread protectors and guide them over the journal as the piston crown is being tapped. As the thread protectors straddle the journal, take a look at the position of the connecting rod and straighten it so that it will come into contact with the journal absolutely square on.

Caution! - The crankshaft **must** not to be turned at this point. The reason for this is that the bearing shells are still 'spread' and are not assuming the correct shape. Damage to the

Positions of the feeler gauges when the bolts are being torqued.

bearing shell surfaces can result from crank rotation.

With the thread protectors removed and the oiled cap fitted to the connecting rod, place a feeler gauge, of the maximum size that can be accommodated, between the connecting rod and the side of the crankshaft and then proceed to torque the adjacent nut or bolt. Each piston and connecting rod is fitted and torqued individually so that any problems associated with fitting that particular piston and connecting rod are isolated and known immediately.

The reason for placing a feeler gauge between the cap and the side of the journal (adjacent to the nut or bolt being torqued) is to prevent the bearing shells being subjected to twisting torque as the nuts are tightened. Without the feeler gauge present the actual bearing shells are forced against the crankshaft journal and this is not desirable.

The crankshaft can be rotated once the connecting rod nuts or bolts have been fully torqued and the feeler

This connecting rod and piston have the minimum amount of side clearance allowable.

gauge removed. After each connecting rod has been fitted, turn the crankshaft over a few times with a torque wrench and note the maximum reading.

After the last piston and connecting rod have been fitted, turn the crankshaft using a torque wrench and note the highest reading. Expect this reading to be between 6-7ft.lb.

Double-check the notches or numbers on the tops of the pistons to ensure each piston is correctly orientated and in the correct bore. Check each connecting rod and cap for matching numbers on the same side as each other. Check that the connecting rod numbers are adjacent to the numbers as stamped on the block rails (if this extra precaution was carried out). Check that each connecting rod small end has a minimum side clearance between it and the piston wrist pin bosses of 0.040in/1.0mm. This completes fitting of the pistons and connecting rods into the block.

Chapter 15
Camshaft & ignition timing marks

With the crankshaft, pistons, connecting rods and timing chain fitted there are several things that are checked at this point and adjusted if necessary. This is the time to check the top dead centre position of number one cylinder in relation to the original factory timing marks, and to mark the crankshaft pulley for camshaft timing and ignition timing points.

All engines have a Top Dead Centre (TDC) mark on the front pulley and an adjacent pointer or degree scale. On standard engines the degrees of advance from TDC will be indicated by marks on the crankshaft pulley (single line pointer on the engine) or by a degree scale fixed to the front of the engine (only one mark on the crankshaft pulley). So there are two ways of achieving the same basic thing.

For high-performance engines the ignition advance degree markings seldom need to be more than 40 degrees in two degree increments or, if

the idle advance requirements of the engine and the total advance degree requirements are known, the exact number of degrees can be marked on to the front pulley or the scale fixed to the front of the engine.

The camshaft degree markings can be set for the full lift position, the opening and closing points of the valves or the exhaust opening point and the inlet closing point.

Note that if you are intending to create a considerable number of degree marks and your engine is of a type with a single pulley mark and a degree scale, you'll need to use the TDC point on the scale (once it's been checked) as if it were a pointer. All new marks will be added to the pulley.

CHECKING TOP DEAD CENTRE

The first thing to check is TDC as every other mark stems from this and, if the TDC mark is wrong, so are all of

the others.

Using a dial indicator and a magnetic stand or a clamp, bring the piston of number one cylinder (the cylinder nearest the front of the engine) to TDC by rotating the crankshaft clockwise: stop immediate the indicator needle first stops. Using fine felt tipped pen, mark the front pulley in line with the pointer (or, if applicable, the degree scale in line with the mark on the pulley). Then rotate the crankshaft anticlockwise an stop immediately the dial indicator needle first stops. Mark this point also on the front pulley or degree scale. The factory marked TDC point will usually be dead in the middle of the two lines you've marked. This procedure should be carried out a few times before the damper/degree scale is permanently marked just to be sure that you've found true TDC.

This method is very accurate, but not dead accurate, because although the piston stops at TDC, further

Number one cylinder at TDC. The dial indicator is registering the highest point of piston travel. Pointer in line with TDC groove in the crankshaft pulley.

Dial indicator needle at the prescribed point BTDC. Pointer is to the right of the groove in the crankshaft pulley. Mark the crankshaft pulley in line with the fixed pointer.

Dial indicator needle at the prescribed point ATDC. Pointer is to the left of the groove in the crankshaft pulley. Mark the crankshaft pulley in line with the fixed pointer.

crankshaft rotation can take place before the piston moves again. To remove this factor from the equation the following procedure can be used. Zero the dial indicator at TDC and then choose a point on the dial indicator just short of the maximum possible reading (say, 0.003in/ 0.075mm). Rotate the crankshaft clockwise to the chosen point and mark the crankshaft pulley/degree scale. Next turn the engine anti-clockwise to the same point on the dial indicator. The point of stopping is the same, it was just approached from the

opposite direction.

The point in the middle of the two felt tipped pen marks on the front pulley/degree scale is the true top dead centre point.

This same procedure can be carried out using a 'dead stop' instead of a dial indicator and stand. It involves making up a strap using 0.312-0.375in/6-10mm thick by 1in/ 25mm wide mild steel flat bar and drilling two clearance holes in the bar so that the bar can be bolted to the top of the block using cylinder head bolt or stud holes. A third hole is drilled and tapped 5/16in UNF or

6mm metric fine, and a short bolt screwed into it with a nut in place to act as a lock to limit accurately the amount of thread that protrudes from the flat bar. The idea, once again, is to stop the piston's travel some way before TDC when the crank is rotated clockwise and then anti-clockwise to the same point.

If the factory mark is, in fact, dead centre between the two felt tipped pen marks it can be regarded as accurate. If the mark is not aligned it, or the pointer (if applicable), will have to be moved.

If the pointer is a fixed scale on

Dead stop comprises a flat bar with adjustable (via the nut and bolt) stop.

Two lines drawn onto the front pulley. In this case the factory machined TDC line is dead centre between the two temporary lines. This engine's TDC mark is accurate.

the engine with one groove (TDC) in the crankshaft pulley and the positions are not correct, the groove has to be brazed up and repositioned. Many modern engines use a lot of plastic and it is very common for these engines to have the scale in the molding. They are not able to be moved. Earlier engines use fixed scales that were cast into the aluminium front cover or metal pressings that were bolted or spot welded onto the engine.

The pointer, if applicable, may be made of steel, in which case it can be heated and bent over slightly to realign the timing point.

In all cases the crankshaft pulley can be removed from the engine, the original groove/s brazed up and new ones cut into the rim of the pulley. The new groove/s can be cut into the rim with a hacksaw or hand filed using a needle file or a narrow-edged file.

IGNITION TIMING MARKS

With the true top dead centre position definitely known, the necessary extra ignition timing marks can be marked on to the crankshaft pulley or front cover. There are two sets of markings for ignition timing; the static/idle speed degree marks and the total advance degree marks. The idle speed ignition timing marks will need to be 12, 14 16 and 18 degrees BTDC (before top dead centre) in two degree increments. This will cover the requirements of most four cylinder engines.

The total advance ignition timing marks can be placed on the crankshaft pulley starting at 30, 32, 34, 36 and finally 38 degrees. This will cover the requirements of most four cylinder engines. If the total advance degree is known at this point, place only that degree marking as this will avoid a clutter of lines and numbers.

Please note that in-depth information on building a high performance ignition system, distributor modifications and optimizing ignition timing to suit any four stroke engine can be found in another Veloce Publishing Speedpro Series book - *How To Build & Power Tune Distributor-Type Ignition Systems* also by Des Hammill.

CAMSHAFT TIMING MARKS

For camshaft timing the camshaft manufacturer's listed opening and closing points of the inlet and exhaust can be used, as can the full lift position of the number one cylinder's inlet valve (a common method). Pushrod engines and single overhead camshaft engines, for example, have a single camshaft with fixed phasing of the inlet and exhaust events. The inlet valve

timing of number one cylinder is used for full lift timing, or the opening and closing points of the inlet cycle are used. Either way, the relevant degree points need to be accurately marked on the crankshaft pulley. This means marking the inlet opening point, the inlet closing point and/or the full lift timing point. The full lift point is widely used because it's accurate and makes it easy to set and advance or retard the camshaft timing when required.

For four valve per cylinder twin camshaft engines, for instance, it's frequently very important in terms of extracting the best possible power from the engine, to know when the inlet valve closes and the point that the exhaust valve opens and forget everything else. The position being that, with such efficient cylinder heads the exhaust valves can and should be opened as late as possible as this relates directly to the torque produced by the engine (piston is under pressure for as long as possible), yet not opened so late as to restrict expulsion of the exhaust gases from the cylinder before the piston starts to rise. Consider 70 degrees BBDC to be the earliest point of opening for engines turning up to 8000rpm, 75 degrees for engines turning up to 9000rpm and 80 degrees for any engine of this type. The latest that the inlet should ever close on this type of engine is 80 degrees ABDC and 70 degrees ABDC the earliest that the inlet valve needs to close. After choosing the camshafts for the application, time them on the basis of exhaust opening and inlet closing only.

Most camshaft manufacturers and suppliers provide full information on their products in the form of a 'card.' Some 'cam cards' come with a minimum of information but it is usually enough. For example. a 'cam card' may list only the following:

Inlet Opens 37 Degrees Before Top Dead Centre.

Inlet Closes 75 Degrees After Bottom Dead Centre.

Exhaust Opens 75 Degrees Before Bottom Dead Centre.

Exhaust Closes 37 Degrees After Top Dead Centre.

Full Lift Inlet 108 After Top Dead Centre.

Valve Lift 0.450in - Duration 290 Degrees - Mechanical.

In such a case certain other information can be calculated such as the full lift position. This involves dividing the advertised duration by two and then deducting the inlet opening number of degrees from that figure. This gives 108 degrees, which is, on a symmetrically ground camshaft, the full lift position. If in doubt, check with the camshaft manufacturer or grinder.

With the above information used as an example (the crankshaft pulley already has true TDC, 12, 14, 16 and 18 degrees BTDC, 30, 32, 34, 36 and 38 degrees BTDC marked) the 37 degrees BTDC timing will not need to be marked as the ignition timing marks can be used, but 108 degrees ATDC for the full lift timing, and 75 degrees ABTDC for the inlet closing point will need to be marked on the pulley. In addition to this, the exhaust events should be included as this will enable the camshaft phasing to be checked out, to avoid a clutter of timing marks on the circumference of the crankshaft pulley, they are not usually included.

On single camshaft engines the full lift timing position is definitely the best option in terms of accuracy and expediency.

DEGREE MARKING THE CRANKSHAFT PULLEY

To mark the crankshaft pulley it must be removed from the engine. In preparation for marking the pulley the following will be required. A white piece of paper or cardboard about 12in by 12in/300mm by 300mm, a 360 degree protractor, a 12in/300mm ruler, a pair of compasses and a pencil or ball point pen.

Mark the centre of the paper and then measure the diameter of the damper. Using compasses set to the radius of the damper diameter, draw a circle on the paper from the centre point.

Next, using the ruler, draw a line through the centre of the circle with the lines extending 1inch/25mm, or so, beyond the circle: mark the top of the line TDC and the bottom of the line BDC.

Note that the pulley is going to be placed face down on to the paper which will mean that, from now on, all degree markings are going to be drawn on to the paper in reverse. However, the figures will transpose from the paper to the pulley correctly.

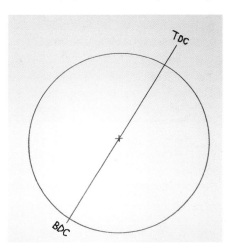

Paper with the diameter of the damper and a straight line (indicating TDC & BDC) bisecting the centre drawn on it.

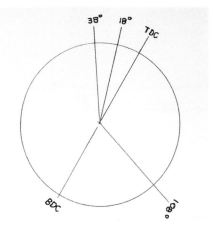

All relevant degree markings accurately placed around the circumference of the circle on the paper.

Place a protractor in the centre of the circle and set the 0 degree point on the TDC line. Moving anti-clockwise from TDC, mark 12, 14, 16 and 18 degrees, then move around to the 30 degree point and mark 30, 32, 34, 36, 38 degrees. Continue on around to mark the necessary camshaft event degree points.

Note that some camshaft manufacturers list camshaft timings at 0.050in/0.25mm lifter rise for the accurate timing of the opening and closing points. If this is the case with your camshaft, substitute the 0.050in/0.25mm lifter rise figures for the opening and closing points of the number one cylinder inlet timing events. These figures are very accurate and quite similar to use in the final analysis. The 0.050in/0.25mm lifter rise factor has no effect and does not apply to the full lift timing position method (another advantage).

The reason some camshaft manufacturers use 0.050in/0.25mm lifter rise figures is that the absolute opening and closing points to 0.001in/0.028mm accuracy can be difficult to determine. Using the 0.050in/0.25mm point is more convenient and accurate but is still not as convenient as using

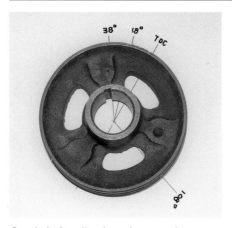

Crankshaft pulley face down on the paper, ready to have the degree points transferred to it.

A crankshaft pulley that has been marked with extra degree marks and has the numbers and letters neatly in line under the timing marks.

Crankshaft pulley held in a vice, the various degree marks being hand filed in its rim. Paint the crankshaft pulley black and fill the grooves with white paint for clarity.

the inlet full lift position of the number one cylinder.

The damper can now be placed face down on to the piece of paper so that the TDC line of the damper is in line with the line on the paper and the damper is concentric with the circle drawn on the paper.

At this stage all degree points on the paper are in true alignment with the crankshaft pulley and can be transferred to it. After all points have been carefully marked on the pulley rim, check that the original TDC mark on the damper is still in line with the TDC line on the drawing and that the pulley is concentric with the drawn circle. Then double-check all of the

degree markings to make sure that they are all perfectly in line with the drawing's degree points.

The marks can be made permanent by very carefully cutting them into the crankshaft pulley rim using a needle file or hacksaw. File/ saw each mark very lightly at first, then check that it is dead accurate before increasing its depth to 0.040in/0.1mm. This method is quite acceptable if carried out correctly.

The corresponding numbers and letters are then stamped or engraved onto the surface of the pulley so that there is no confusion now, or later, as to what each degree mark is for. This can be difficult on some pulleys where the numbers can't be accommodated on the rim and may have to be placed on the face.

CHECKING CAMSHAFT TIMING (IN-BLOCK CAMS)

With marking of the crankshaft pulley completed, the camshaft timing is now checked against these marks. This process may require some repetitive work because, after the timing has been checked and the timing proves to be out (a most likely scenario), the

crankshaft pulley and the front cover of the engine have to be removed and then accurately refitted every time the camshaft timing is altered and rechecked.

An alternative to having to remove the timing cover to adjust camshaft timing is to modify the timing cover so that the front of the camshaft sprocket or, more specifically, the sprocket securing nuts, are able to be got at while the engine is fully assembled. Most timing covers can be modified to allow for easy camshaft position changes. When the timing cover has been so modified the camshaft timing can usually be altered in a few minutes.

The camshaft drive sprocket needs to be adjustable (readily available for popular engines) or be made adjustable. If the standard sprocket is to be made adjustable the drive dowel slot in the sprocket is elongated so that the camshaft can be advanced (camshaft timing seldom needs to be retarded). The securing bolt holes in the sprocket also need to be elongated to allow for the radial movement of the camshaft drive sprocket.

With in-block camshafts, the best way of timing the camshaft at this point is by using the full lift timing method. Opening and closing point checking really requires the cylinder head to be fitted to avoid unnecessary complication. To time an engine using the full lift timing method, a reasonably close fitting rod will have to be inserted down through the top of the block (not a push rod) to make contact with the lifter. The rod has to be able to be inserted and withdrawn from the top of the block.

The top of the rod should be proud of the block deck and a dial indicator set up to read its vertical movement. The dial indicator is set to

A modified camshaft cover with a removable plate secured by four small nuts.

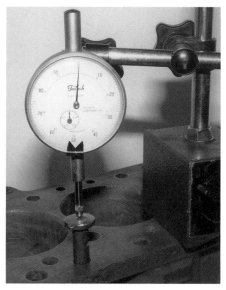

Rod in a block with the dial indicator on zero.

Dial indicator showing 0.030in before the needle reaches zero.

Line on the pulley is to the left of the TDC mark.

Line on the pulley is to the right of TDC mark.

ro at the point of full lift and then the crankshaft is rotated clockwise to a point 0.003in/0.075mm before the full lift point and the crankshaft pulley temporarily marked in line with the pointer.

The crankshaft is then turned further clockwise to the full lift point and on until the 0.030in/0.75mm point is picked up again. The difference being, of course, that this is the other side of the 'toe' of the camshaft. Slight hand pressure (carefully applied) may well be required on the rod to ensure that the follower and rod faithfully follow the camshaft profile. When the 0.030in/0.75mm point is reached again the crankshaft pulley is marked in line with the pointer.

The two temporary lines will be either side of the 108 degree (for the example camshaft previously described) line marked on the crankshaft pulley and if the camshaft timing is 'dead on' the gaps between the three lines will be equal. If the gaps are not equal the camshaft has to be moved in relation to the crankshaft.

This is achieved by turning the engine anti-clockwise and coming back up to the full lift point. Undo the camshaft to camshaft sprocket bolts and turn the crankshaft until the 108

degree mark on the crankshaft pulley lines up with the pointer on the engine. The securing bolts of the camshaft sprocket are then tightened and the full checking procedure repeated. The camshaft timing is correct when the gaps between the lines are equal.

The reason for checking the camshaft timing (as opposed to just fitting the camshaft and timing chain) and then repositioning it if necessary, is that the engine will not produce optimum power unless the camshaft is at the very least timed to the manufacturer's specifications. Some engines also respond to the camshaft being set advanced or retarded in relation to the manufacturer's settings.

Note that the camshaft can be timed using a degree wheel that is bolted on to the front of the crankshaft and a separate pointer rigged up to indicate true TDC. The reason for going to the trouble of marking the crankshaft pulley and using the engine's own TDC marking is simply to make the engine concerned totally self-sufficient for setting and checking

procedures. The whole system is also very rigid and offers excellent repeat use now and in the future.

Frequently, after all of the money

that has been invested in rebuilding the engine has been spent, a relatively simple thing like poor camshaft timing can mean that the engine is considerably down on power. As with all other aspects of the short assembly rebuild, methodical workmanship in conjunction with good information will ensure that everything works in uniso and the full potential of the engine w be realized. Time and patience will b well rewarded.

Chapter 16
Oiling system

STOCK SUMPS (OIL PANS)

e stock sump could have a front,
ar, central or full-length oil reservoir.
ithin the range of a single engine
be there can be several different
mps. At the very least, use the
gest capacity stock sump that will fit
e engine/installation.

Any sump that is to be used on a
gh-performance engine needs to
ve a windage tray with a baffle fitted
it. Some engines have very good
ndage trays fitted as original
uipment and may only need to have
baffle, which will then surround the
pickup, fabricated and fitted to the
y. Usually, there is no windage tray,
baffle, and both must be fabricated
suit the stock sump.

Some manufacturers offer sumps
the higher performance engines in
e same family as your own that
ature increased oil capacity, a
ndage tray and baffling. Using these
rts can be a reasonably inexpensive

way of ensuring that your engine has
adequate oiling. Failing this, if more oil
capacity is required, a suitable sump
will have to be specially fabricated to
suit the application or one of the many
aftermarket sumps designed and built
to suit a wide range of engines/
installations purchased and fitted.

Windage tray & baffle
The oil that is in the sump must be
tranquil oil, not foaming, aerated oil.
This 'tranquility' is achieved using a
windage tray. The windage tray is
placed at oil level and must clear the
lowest point of the crankshaft/
connecting rods/connecting rod bolts
by 0.25in/6mm. The oil is flung off the
crankshaft and, instead of hitting the
oil, hits the metal tray. The oil then
runs back into the oil reservoir of the
sump through holes or slots that are
cut into the tray, or over the edges of
the tray. The oil under the tray is
reasonably tranquil because of the
tray.

Oil must be able to get back
down into the oil reservoir easily -
particularly under high G-forces which
tend to trap oil above the windage tray
- and this means that the windage tray
must not be tight fitting all around the
edges of the sump (it must have a 1/
16-1/8in/1.6-3mm) gap or a series of
holes near the edges). There seems to
be quite a few sumps and windage
trays around that really don't allow
adequate drainage. If oil is trapped
above the tray by high G-forces the
effective oil level will drop significantly
and oil starvation could be the result,
especially on a long, high speed curve.
The problem only shows up under
extreme racing conditions, but this
does not alter the fact that some
windage tray designs are not right.

A windage tray can be fabricated
out of tin plate which is 0.025-
0.028in/0.70-0.79mm thick and is
retained by being sandwiched
between the block rails and the sump
gasket and the sump itself. No welding

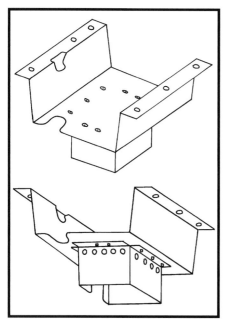

Square baffle pop-riveted to the underside of a windage tray. Note holes near the top of the baffle to prevent the entrapment of air.

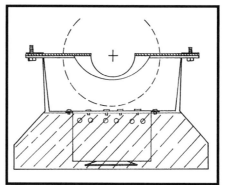

Sectioned diagram of a sump with the crankshaft swing clearly shown, the windage tray and baffle in position and oil level in relation to the crankshaft.

This original equipment windage tray is sandwiched between the block and pressed steel sump.

Rear mounted oil reservoir with increas oil capacity and a specially fabricated windage tray which is sandwiched between the sump gasket and the bloc rails.

is required, but the windage tray must be specially fabricated to suit the engine block and sump concerned. Provision has to be made to clear the various components sharing the sump such as the oil pump and dipstick.

The windage tray should, ideally, be fabricated to compensate for the engine's installed angle so that the actual tray is level with the oil. If the windage tray is made parallel to the crankshaft axis and the engine is installed angled, the oil level is going to be either over the top of the tray at the back of the engine, or there is going to be a gap between the oil at the front of the tray (reduced oil capacity). If the windage tray is awash with oil at the rear, there is always the possibility of the oil being picked up by the crankshaft at some stage. If the windage tray and the oil are level when the vehicle is level and the tray is 0.25in/6mm away from the maximum swing of the crankshaft, it is

not likely that the crankshaft will ever come into contact with the oil.

Fitting a baffle to the underside of the windage tray helps to ensure that the oil pump pickup always has oil around it. This involves shrouding the pickup to a degree to stop excessive movement of the oil around the pickup, but not so much as to prevent oil from getting to the pickup.

The baffle fits down into the oil and serves to reduce the rate of movement of the oil when the engine is subjected to G-forces. The baffle is made square because it's the shape required and it is easy to fabricate and pop rivet on to the windage tray. A series of holes are drilled around the top of the baffle to avoid entrapment of air.

With a stock sump, when a windage tray and baffle combination are fitted, there is a considerable

improvement over the stock system. carefully designed and fitted windag tray improves engine reliability to a remarkable degree, even if the amou of oil held by the sump is not increased, because it makes better u of what is there.

In many instances the amount oil that the stock sump holds is sufficient. For street applications the stock sump capacity is almost alway enough and fabrication of a windage tray and baffle is all that is required.

Increasing oil capacity

Sumps can be altered to increase oil capacity and improve the design to reduce the possibility of oil starvatio The original oil reservoir section can be cut off the sump and a new reservoir fabricated and welded on using a Mig welder (for minimum distortion).

To prevent distortion, the cut p must be mounted on to a bare engir block before the new fabricated reservoir is welded on. If a sump is c and welded without being bolted down to a block, it is extremely unlikely that the finished product wil be oil tight when fitted: it doesn't tak much distortion (0.015-0.030in/0.38 0.78mm) to cause poor fitting of the sump to the block.

Note that increasing the oil capacity of a sump alone does not mean that oil pressure problems will not be experienced. There is more to it than this and a windage tray/baffle must still be fabricated and fitted.

Aluminium sumps

Aftermarket sumps which feature increased oil capacity and a windage tray and baffling are available for the most popular engines only. These cast aluminium sumps are always quite expensive as a result of relatively low volume production runs. The decision to use a readily available cast aluminium aftermarket sump depends on how well it will fit the particular engine installation.

If it is not possible to fit an aftermarket sump into the engine bay, there is often no alternative but to modify the original sump. Original sumps that are cast in aluminium (quite common these days) can be quite successfully modified to suit virtually any application and the new aluminium reservoir will have to be Tig welded to the existing sump. This involves accurate fabrication and welding and, once again, the original sump will still have to be bolted to a mock during welding to preclude distortion.

Windage trays and baffles should be used with these aluminium sumps, too. Fabrication and retention is as previously described.

Single engine specialists frequently offer modified production based sumps to suit 'their' engine.

ENGINE INSTALLATION ANGLE

North/South orientated engines are usually installed in the car at an angle - the rear of the engine being lower than the front. There is not too much that

can be done about this in most instances, but what can be done should be done to level the engine. For instance, the rear transmission mount can be packed up, but not to the point where the gearbox touches the transmission tunnel. The two engine mounts can frequently be lowered, but not to the point where the sump will contact the front crossmember.

In all non-stock vehicles, such as kit cars or conversions, the engine should be installed as level as possible. When an engine is level, the oil level in the sump can often be raised without detriment. With the engine level, maximum oil capacity can be realized without the possibility of oil being 'picked up' by the crankshaft. If the crankshaft contacts the oil, one way or another it will be noticed. Huge amounts of oil smoke will be emitted from the exhaust pipes as the oil rings are overloaded and the engine bay may well be wet with oil.

OIL PUMPS

Stock oil pumps - in first class order - will prove sufficient for all high performance street engines, while uprated stock oil pumps, which have had the relief valve packed to increase oil pressure, will cope with most engine applications using up to 6500rpm when the engine has moderate bearing clearances. Any engine that is going to be subjected to sustained high revs (over 7000rpm) on a regular basis should have a high volume oil pump fitted. Always fit a new oil pump drive, if applicable, at the same time.

Remove the baseplate of the oil pump and check the clearances between the gears and then between the gears and the housing or, on bi-rotors, between the rotor and the

Standard oil pump pick-up which is well supported with stays.

housing and then between the rotors. Check the end clearances between the gears or rotor and the endplate. In all these instances, the minimum clearance (0.002in/0.05mm) is desirable so remove material from the housing if the end clearance is excessive (more than 0.004in/0.01mm) to avoid oil pressure reduction.

On new pumps check the inside of the housing for machining swarf and clean it out if there is any present. Manufacturers are as careful as possible, but there is always a chance that the housing was not cleaned correctly: a simple thing like this can lead to severe engine damage. In the final analysis, it doesn't matter who did or didn't do what and when, the result is the same, engine damage that could have been prevented quite easily by checking and taking no risks.

For instant oil priming on initial start up, the gear cavity or rotor cavity should be completely filled, or as much as is possible, with petroleum jelly. This method is excellent and universally used. Do not rely on the pump to pick up oil immediately if only oil is used to prime the pump. On some engines if petroleum jelly is not used to prime the pump the pump will never pick up oil - no matter how long the engine is turned over.

CRANKCASE VENTILATION

Close piston to bore clearance and well seated rings will reduce the amount of combustion pressure that can get into the crankcase. Engines built to the recommended specifications will still have to vent the disturbed air, caused by the rotating crankshaft assembly, but nothing like that of a large clearanced engine.

The standard type of positive crankcase ventilation system will cope with this well. This involves the usual tube out of a rocker cover or camshaft cover and into the inlet manifold via a one-way valve or an anti-backfire valve. The disadvantage of this system is the amount of oil mist or oil-contaminated air being constantly drawn into the engine via the 3/8in/10mm or 1/2in/12mm inside diameter tube from the rocker cover. Street engines, however, must meet legal requirements and it is not as if such an engine will be fumy, it just needs to be vented.

Oil is often pushed up the tube of the dipstick and out of the engine when any substantial rpm is used. The solution is to seal off the top of the dipstick using a trimmed down suitably sized distributor lead boot. The dipstick should also be held in position using a tension spring. This is to avoid

the dipstick lifting and allowing oil to come out of the engine (no-one likes to see a messy engine or engine compartment or to lose oil unecessarily!)

Competition engines are vented by having a pipe (minimum inside diameter of 5/8in/16mm) coming out of the block from the usual crankcase ventilation take-off point; another pipe coming off the rocker cover and another coming off the front timing cover, with the three pipes going to a catch tank, the inlet points of which are above the highest outlet of the engine. Single or twin overhead camshaft engines have a pipe coming off the block, one pipe for each camshaft and another coming directly from the sump above the oil level (inlet must be shielded from direct oil splash), with the three or four pipes going to a catch tank.

OIL & FILTER

Use the motor oil recommended by the manufacturer to 'run in' the engine. The reason for this is that many engines require oils with different properties because of the valve train design, and to ignore these requirements is folly. Do not use friction modified oils in new engines initially; only use this type of oil after the rings are completely bedded in. There is a wide range of high specification oils available and all appear to be excellent (and

expensive).

Change the oil after the first 500 miles (or sooner) and check the oil that comes out of the engine and the filter element (cut the filter up) for particles and fragments. If fragments and particles are found *en masse* in the oil, something is wrong. **Caution!** Do not run the engine again until the cause has been ascertained and corrected: a partial strip down will be necessary.

If the engine is being subjected to sustained high rpm competition use, change the oil every 250 to 500 miles (the shorter period for dirty/dusty conditions) or any time after the oil temperature has been to the maximum allowable limit. Change the oil at the normal manufacturer recommended intervals in road-going engines. **Caution!** - Check the oil for particles each and every time it is changed.

When changing the engine oil, the oil must be hot and the drain plug must be at the lowest point to ensure **all** of the old oil is drained out. If the engine is in a car, for instance, the car can be jacked up on the opposite side to the drain plug so that the drain plug is at the lowest point.

Original equipment rated oil filters are adequate for 6000-8000rpm. Higher flowing aftermarket filters are available, but they should not be necessary unless you're going over 8000rpm. Fit the best oil filter available.

Chapter 17
Conclusion

The information from a workshop manual specific to your engine will give all torque wrench settings and factory recommended clearances. Many manuals feature exploded view diagrams and pictures that can be very helpful to the assembler when putting a particular engine together. Most libraries have a good range of manuals that cover all mass-production in-line four cylinder engines and cover the design features peculiar to that engine. This book is non-specific in that respect as it deals with the overall technique of blueprinting, optimising clearances and reducing friction in any four cylinder in-line engine.

There are always peculiarities that apply to a particular engine and a specific workshop manual is an excellent source of information.

It is recommended that a new water pump be fitted to any modified engine, and the radiator uprated so that the chances of overheating the engine are reduced to a minimum. Modified engines almost always produce more heat than stock engines. Cast iron cylinder heads do not dissipate the heat as well as aluminium cylinder heads. To prevent overspeeding of the water pump on a high revving engine, the pulley can be increased in diameter by 20 to 30 per cent.

All engines should be run with a thermostat or a restricter plate. The thermostat works to warm up the engine in the shortest possible time, while the restricter plate will take about three times as long to do the same thing, depending on the size of the hole (determined by testing, but often about 25mm/1in diameter). Suffice to say that a certain sized hole will allow the particular engine to attain a certain running temperature overall. If overheating problems are experienced, the hole can be enlarged to allow a reduction in the usual engine operating temperature of, say, 10 degrees. Conversely, running an engine too cold is going to cause excessive bore wear (smaller hole required). The ideal temperature is as hot as possible without risk of overheating. Consider 70-80 degrees C/158-176 degrees F about right for a high-performance engine. Engines equipped with a thermostat that jams in the closed position are generally ruined and it is because of this factor that thermostats are often removed. Many racing engines simply have the thermostat removed and, because of the limited use they receive, bore wear is not a significant factor.

Caution! - All performance engine installations should have a fire extinguisher fitted to the vehicle. An engine fire must be put out quickly and the fire extinguisher must be of sufficient capacity to do this (2lb/0.90kg minimum).

STARTING AND RUNNING IN A REBUILT ENGINE

Caution! - **Don't** use a friction modified oil in a newly built engine. The reason for this is that, whilst these oils are excellent for 'run in' engines (engines with rings that are well and truly seated), they will prevent new rings from seating properly and bore glazing will be the result. The engine will have high oil consumption which can only be remedied by honing the bores and fitting new rings, which means an engine strip down.

Fill the engine with oil to the full level and then add 0.25in/6mm more: this extra oil will be used to fill the filter. Note that once the engine is fully primed, oil will usually have to be added to get the level to the full mark on the dipstick **before** the engine is 'fired up.'

When the engine was assembled, the oil pump will have been packed with petroleum jelly. This means the pump is effectively primed and starts pumping oil around the engine from the first revolution of the crankshaft.

With the engine full of oil and all of the sparkplugs removed, it can be turned over on the starter. Usually the oil pressure gauge will start moving within about 10 or 15 seconds and be at a constant pressure within 20 to 25 seconds. With the sparkplugs removed the engine is free to turn without compression and will turn the highest cranking speed possible on the starter. Note that when the oil has filled the galleries it then comes under pressure and the starter motor will be heard to slow. At this point, the pressure gauge will begin to show a reading.

Caution! - The engine **must** be primed with oil before it is started. This means that there must be at least 25psi/172kpa or more oil pressure present. Fitting a good quality oil pressure gauge is mandatory for a performance orientated engine.

Caution! - Fit the air cleaner to the engine before starting it. If the ignition is not correctly set the engine could backfire, which could lead to an engine fire. Always have on hand a fire extinguisher which is ready for instant use.

With the sparkplugs refitted, the engine can be cranked over with a view to starting. Use a well charged battery and consider using an 'engine start' spray (containing petroleum distillate) to ensure that the engine fires immediately. Priming the fuel system with the petroleum distillate mixture from a spray can will avoid prolonged cranking of the starter.

With a small amount of throttle applied via the idle adjustment screw, start the engine. The engine should run at a speed of between 1500-2000rpm: not at idle speed as this is too low on some engines to produce good oil pressure and insufficient oil will be splashed around inside the crankcase to lube those parts that are splash fed. Racing engines may need slightly higher rpm because of the camshafts fitted (reluctant to idle, and poor low end performance). Monitor the engine for oil leaks once it is running.

The engine rpm should be varied between 1500 and 2000rpm while the water comes up to operating temperature. Once the water temperature is up to about 180 degrees F/80 degrees C, turn the engine off and let it cool down **completely**.

Check the oil and water levels.

When the engine is next started the ignition timing must be set using a strobe light. Any engine with a high performance type of camshaft fitted is going to need from 10 to 16 degrees BTDC of idle ignition timing. Retarded engines overheat and are generally quite sluggish and over-advanced engines are hard to start (kick back) and 'pink' under normal acceleration or when subjected to increased engine load.

With the engine inspected for oil leaks and the water level checked, the engine must be subjected to load conditions, but note that anything over 3500rpm is to be avoided. A street machine needs to be got on to the highway and into top gear as quickly as possible and the engine speed varied between 2000 and 3000rpm. This entails holding the engine rpm at a steady 2000rpm and accelerating the engine up to 3000 using up to three-quarter throttle and then, as soon as 3000rpm is reached, allowing the engine to slow back down to 2000rpm. Using this 'running in' method the engine is subjected to acceleration load (piston rings under pressure) without excessive rpm being used: the cycle is repeated over and over. This process can get a bit monotonous, but it does serve to 'bed' the rings in reasonably quickly without the possibility of overheating the internal engine components. After ten minutes running like this the engine can be stopped and allowed to cool down **completely** which will take about an hour. Not all types of piston ring sets need this sort of treatment, but it does ensure that the rings (irrespective of type) will be efficiently 'run in.'

New pistons (especially standard type cast pistons running with close piston to bore clearances) 'settle' or stabilize through being heated up from cold to normal operating temperature and then being allowed to cool completely: the more times the pistons are heated and cooled **before** the engine is subjected to full loading and high rpm, the better.

When engines are new and being 'run in' they generate more heat than after they are 'run in,' which makes the initial running a critical time. If a new engine is subjected to excessive heat build-up before the pistons are stabilised, the engine may seize a piston or two (piston skirt to bore contact).

With any new engine installation there are invariably 'teething' problems. During the first few runs of the engine do not venture too far and carry sufficient tools to effect minor adjustments.

Caution! - If there is an engine problem, stop the engine to investigate and find out exactly what is happening. **Do not** be tempted to run the engine just to get back to your starting point - serious engine damage could be the result.

The engine will need a minimum of ten of these ten minute sessions - with complete cooling down in between.

Avoid high rpm for 500 miles/800km. Check the air/fuel mixture ratio before using high rpm and monitor the coolant temperature constantly. Racing engines seldom get this amount of running in and, as a consequence, there is some risk of seizure.

CHECKING USED OIL & THE FILTER

Once the engine is in service inspect the oil and contents of the filter when they are removed from the engine at **every** oil and filter change. **Caution!** - On a 'new' road-going engine, change the oil and filter after the first 500 miles, or sooner. Change the oil and filter on a competition engine every 500 racing miles. Check the oil level in a racing engine after every race for level and discolouration (water

contamination). **Caution!** - Find the true cause of any problem before using the engine again.

The oil can be drained into a large clean pan; once the oil has settled, carefully drain off the bulk to leave 1/4 inch/6mm, or so, in the bottom of the pan. The remaining oil can then be checked for fragments. The type of fragments can vary from bearing material to aluminium, steel or cast iron. If any type of fragment is found, further investigation is required to ascertain exactly where it has come from. This will require the removal of the sump and a general inspection of the likely components. If necessary, remove the engine.

Simple things that are not attended to early enough can destroy an engine. The presence of fragments means metal to metal contact is occuring and it will just continue until there is a mechanical failure. Most major engine failures of this nature are preventable if the engine is inspected on a regular basis. Admittedly, there will more than likely be some engine damage if fragments are found in the oil, but the engine is not ruined completely at this point. The situation may well require the engine to be removed and partially or completely stripped down. It is nearly always far cheaper to replace offending parts and restore the engine to A1 condition rather than run the engine until it is beyond repair.

The filter can be cut up using tin snips and the inside of the filter canister thoroughly checked for any particles and fragments. The actual filter material can be visually checked for particles by separating the folds. If there is a problem in an engine the resulting fragments and particles invariably end up in the oiling system, so the used oil and filter are the logical things to check in the first instance.

ENGINE INSPECTION WITH SUMP (OIL PAN) REMOVED

A great deal of the internal engine componentry can be checked by visual inspection and checking for excessive movement once the sump has been removed. An example of this is checking for excessive big end movement by hand (with good clearances there is no perceptible movement radially on the journal: there will be endfloat).

The floor of the sump can be checked to see if there are any metal particles resting on it. Most engines end up with a thin layer of 'sludge' on the floor of the pan and this is acceptable, but it **must** be washed out completely before the pan goes back on to the engine.

The majority of internal components can be checked for things such as deterioration of connecting rod bearings (cap removal) and main bearings (cap removal), timing chain wear (if fitted in the block) connecting rod bolt or nut tension (check nut or bolt torque and, perhaps, bolt length if the details are available), connecting rod side clearance (feeler gauge measurement), thrust bearing clearance on the mains (feeler gauge measurement), piston skirt breakage (visual inspection), underside of the piston crown and excess clearances of the main and big end bearings (score marks on the shells obvious signs of wear).

POSTSCRIPT

When in-line four cylinder engines are rebuilt correctly to suit a particular purpose they invariably give excellent service with reliability. Any engine is only as strong as its weakest component (usually the connecting rods) and the limit of most components is determined by engine speed. The engine cannot be expected to go beyond a reasonable speed without the possibility of mechanical failure being taken into account. Many factory performance engines are equipped with excellent parts direct from the manufacturer and are, basically, 'bullet proof': however, even they must be maintained correctly if failure is to be avoided. No engine can survive without maintenance. Good maintenance and frequent checking of components and replacement is **essential** if you are to get the best overall results out of an engine. The harder the service the engine is subjected to the more frequent the maintenance must be and the more rigid the standards must be. **Leave nothing to chance on an engine used for competition**.

LSO FROM VELOCE PUBLISHING -

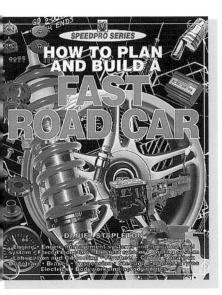

HOW TO PLAN AND BUILD A FAST ROAD CAR
By Daniel Stapleton

ISBN 1 874105 60 X.
Price £15.99*

book in the *SpeedPro* series.

For those wanting to make their go car ister the choice of components and iodifications is bewildering - here, at ist, is a straightforward guide.

How to improve all four aspects of car erformance - acceleration, braking, top peed and cornering speed - without asting money.

Clear, understandable style, with over 00 photos/illustrations.

Applies to any road car.

Contains useful addresses and contacts.

An indispensable guide for *anyone* lanning to modify their car for higher erformance.

• Daniel Stapleton has written a number of magazine articles and books on the subject of high performance tuning/modification.

CONTENTS
Engine • Engine management systems and ignition • Fuel system • Forced induction • Exhaust systems • Cooling systems • Engine lubrication and oil cooling • Flywheel and clutch • Gearbox • Drivetrain • Brakes • Suspension and steering • Wheels and tyres • Electrics & instruments • Bodywork and aerodynamics • Index

SPECIFICATION
Paperback. 250 x 207mm (portrait). 128 pages. Over 200 mono photographs/illustrations.

RETAIL SALES
Veloce books are stocked by or can be ordered from bookshops and specialist mail order companies. In case of difficulty we can supply direct (credit cards accepted).

* *Price subject to change.*

Veloce Publishing Ltd., 33 Trinity Street, Dorchester, Dorset DT1 1TT, England. Tel: 01305 260068/Fax: 01305 268864/ E-mail: veloce@veloce.co.uk

Visit Veloce on the Web - www.veloce.co.uk

ALSO FROM VELOCE PUBLISHING -

HOW TO BUILD & POWER TUNE WEBER & DELLORTO DCOE & DHLA CARBURETORS
- 3rd edition

by Des Hammill

ISBN 1 903706 75 0
Price £17.99*

A book in the **SpeedPro** series. All you could want to know about the world's most famous and popular high-performance sidedraught carburetors. Strip & rebuild. Tuning. Jetting. Choke sizes. Application formula gives the right set-up for *your* car. Covers all Weber DCOE & Dellorto DHLA carburetors.

CONTENTS
COMPONENT IDENTIFICATION: The anatomy of DCOE & DHLA carburetors • DISMANTLING: Step-by-step advice on dismantling. Assessing component serviceability • DIFFICULT PROCEDURES: Expert advice on overcoming common problems in mechanical procedure • ASSEMBLY: Step-by-step advice on assembly. Fuel filters. Ram tubes.

Fuel pressure • SETTING UP: Choosing the right jets and chokes to get the best performance from *your* engine • FITTING CARBURETORS & SYNCHRONISATION: Covers alignment with manifold and balancing airflow • FINAL TESTING & ADJUSTMENTS: Dyno and road testing. Solving low rpm problems. Solving high rpm problems. Re-tuning.

THE AUTHOR
Des Hammill has a background in precision engineering and considers his ability to work very accurately a prime asset. Des has vast experience of building racing engines on a professional basis and really does know how to get the most out of a Weber or Dellorto carburetor. Having lived and worked in many countries around the world, Des currently splits

his time between the UK and Ne[w] Zealand.

SPECIFICATION
Softback • 250 x 207mm (portrait) 96 pages • Over 100 black & whit[e] photographs and line illustrations.

RETAIL SALES
Veloce books are stocked by or ca[n] be ordered from bookshops and spe[-] cialist mail order companies. Alterna[-] tively, Veloce can supply direct (cred[it] cards accepted).

* Price subject to change.

Veloce Publishing Ltd, 33 Trini[ty] Street, Dorchester, Dorset DT1 1T[T] England. Tel: 01305 260068/Fa[x] 01305 268864.

Visit Veloce on the Web - www.veloce.co.uk

ALSO FROM VELOCE PUBLISHING -

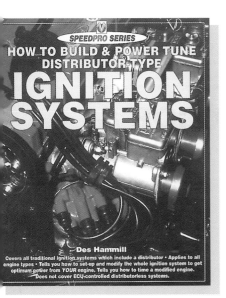

HOW TO BUILD & POWER TUNE DISTRIBUTOR-TYPE IGNITION SYSTEMS
by Des Hammill

ISBN 1 903706 91 2
Price £13.99*

A book in the **SpeedPro** series. Expert practical advice from an experienced race engine builder on how to build an ignition system that delivers maximum power reliably. A lot of rubbish is talked about ignition systems and there's a bewildering choice of expensive aftermarket parts which all claim to deliver more power. Des Hammill cuts through the myth and hyperbole and tells readers what *really* works, so that they can build an excellent system without wasting money on parts and systems that simply don't deliver.

Ignition timing and advance curves for modified engines is another minefield for the inexperienced, but Des uses his expert knowledge to tell readers how to optimise the ignition timing of *any* high-performance engine.

The book applies to all four-stroke gasoline/petrol engines with distributor-type ignition systems, including those using electronic ignition modules: it does not cover engines controlled by ECUs (electronic control units).

CONTENTS
Why modified engines need more idle speed advance • Static idle speed advance setting • Estimating total advance settings • Vacuum advance • Ignition timing marks • Distributor basics • Altering rate of advance • Setting total advance • Quality of spark •

THE AUTHOR
Des Hammill has a background in precision engineering and considers his ability to work very accurately a prime asset. Des has vast experience of building racing engines on a professional basis. Having lived and worked in many countries around the world, he currently splits his time between the UK and New Zealand.

SPECIFICATION
Softback • 250 x 207mm (portrait) • 64 pages • Over 70 black & white photographs and line illustrations.

RETAIL SALES
Veloce books are stocked by or can be ordered from bookshops and specialist mail order companies. Alternatively, Veloce can supply direct (credit cards accepted).

* Price subject to change.

Veloce Publishing Ltd., 33 Trinity Street, Dorchester, Dorset DT1 1TT, England. Tel: 01305 260068/Fax: 01305 268864.

Visit Veloce on the Web - www.veloce.co.uk

SPEEDPRO SERIES

ALSO FROM VELOCE PUBLISHING -

A book in the **SpeedPro** series.

• The complete practical guide to successfully modifying cylinder heads for maximum power, economy and reliability.
• Understandable language and clear illustrations.
• Avoids wasting money on modifications that don't work.
• Applies to almost every car/ motorcycle (does not apply to 2-stroke engines).
• Applies to road and track applications.
• Peter Burgess is a professional

HOW TO BUILD, MODIFY & POWER TUNE CYLINDER HEADS
- Updated & Revised Edition

by Peter Burgess & David Gollan

ISBN 1 903706 76 9
Price £16.99*

race engine builder. David Gollan B ENG HONS is a professional engineer.

CONTENTS
Horsepower and torque • Equipment and tools • Airflow • Building a flowbench • Porting • Valves, valve seats and inserts, valve guides, valve springs • Unleaded fuel conversion • Fuel economy • Includes an overview of camshafts, exhaust systems, ignition, cylinder blocks • Case studies of a selection of popular cylinder heads • Index.

SPECIFICATION
Paperback. 250 x 207mm (portrait). 112 pages. 150 black and white photographs/line illustrations.

RETAIL SALES
Veloce books are stocked by or can be ordered from bookshops and specialist mail order companies. Alternatively, Veloce can supply direct (credit cards accepted).

* Price subject to change.

Veloce Publishing Ltd., 33 Trinity Street, Dorchester, Dorset DT1 1TT England. Tel: 01305 260068/Fax 01305 268864.

Visit Veloce on the Web - www.veloce.co.uk

ALSO FROM VELOCE PUBLISHING -

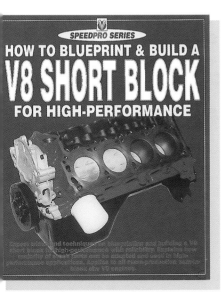

HOW TO BLUEPRINT & BUILD A V8 SHORT BLOCK FOR HIGH PERFORMANCE
by Des Hammill

ISBN 1 874105 70 7
Price £13.99*

A book in the **SpeedPro** series. Expert practical advice from an experienced race engine builder on how to build a V8 short engine block for high performance use using mainly stock parts - including crankshaft and rods. A short block built using Des' techniques will be able to deliver serious high performance with real reliability.

Applies to all sizes and makes of V8 engine with overhead valves operated by pushrods.

CONTENTS
Selecting a suitable short block • Stripdown • Checking critical sizes • Choosing replacement (including non-stock) parts • Cleaning of block & parts • Checking condition of all parts • Crack testing • Remachining • Balancing • Camshaft & lifters • 'Check fitting' engine build technique • Bearing crush • Final rebuild • Checking true top dead centre • Additional degree markings for camshaft & ignition timing • ACcurate camshaft timing • oil pan requirements.

THE AUTHOR
Des Hammill has a background in precision engineering and places great emphasis on accuracy. Des has vast experience of building all types of engine for many categories of motor racing. Having lived in many countries around the world, Des and his wife, Alison, currently live in Devon, England.

SPECIFICATION
Softback •250 x 207mm (portrait) • 112 pages • over 180 black & white photographs & line illustrations.

RETAIL SALES
Veloce books are stocked by or can be ordered from bookshops and specialist mail order companies. Alternatively, Veloce can supply direct (credit cards accepted).

* Price subject to change.

Veloce Publishing Ltd., 33 Trinity Street, Dorchester, Dorset DT1 1TT, England. Tel: 01305 260068/Fax: 01305 268864.

Visit Veloce on the Web - www.veloce.co.uk

SPEEDPRO SERIES

ALSO FROM VELOCE PUBLISHING -

HOW TO CHOOSE CAMSHAFTS & TIME THEM FOR MAXIMUM POWER
by Des Hammill

ISBN 1 903706 59 9
Price £12.99*

A book in the *SpeedPro* series.

Explains in simple language how to choose the right camshaft/s for *YOUR* application and how to find the camshaft timing which gives maximum performance.
• Also explained are all aspects of camshaft design and the importance of lobe phasing, duration & lift.
• Applies to all 4-stroke car-type engines with 4, 5, 6 or 8 cylinders.
• Des Hammill is an engineer and a professional race engine builder with many years of experience.
• Avoids wasting money on modifications that don't work.
• Applies to road and track applications.

CONTENTS
Introduction • Using This Book & Essen-

tial Information • Chapter 1: Terminology • Chapter 2: Choosing the Right Amount of Duration • Chapter 3: Checking Camshafts • Chapter 4: Camshaft Timing Principles • Chapter 5: Camshaft Problems • Chapter 6: Timing Procedure - Cam-in-Block Engines • Chapter 7: Camshaft Timing Procedure - S.O.H.C. Engines • Chapter 8: Camshaft Timing Procedure - T.O.H.C. Engines • Chapter 9: Engine Testing • Index.

THE AUTHOR
Des Hammill has a background in precision engineering and places great emphasis on accuracy. Des has vast experience of building all types of engine for many categories of motor racing. Having lived in many countries around the world, Des and his wife, Alison, currently live in Devon, England.

SPECIFICATION
Softback • 250 x 207mm (portrait) • 6◌
pages • 150 black & white photograph
& line illustrations.

RETAIL SALES

Veloce books are stocked by or can b◌
ordered from bookshops and speciali◌
mail order companies. Alternatively
Veloce can supply direct (credit car◌
accepted).

* Price subject to change.

Veloce Publishing Ltd., 33 Trinity Stree
Dorchester, Dorset DT1 1TT, Englan◌
Tel: 01305 260068/Fax: 01305 26886◌
E-mail: veloce@veloce.co.uk

Visit Veloce on the Web - www.veloce.co.uk

Index

SPEED**PRO** SERIES

Visit Veloce on the Web - www.veloce.co.uk